Library Problems in Science and Technology

Bowker Series in
PROBLEM-CENTERED APPROACHES TO LIBRARIANSHIP
Thomas J. Galvin, Series Editor

CURRENT PROBLEMS IN REFERENCE SERVICE
by Thomas J. Galvin
PROBLEMS IN SCHOOL MEDIA MANAGEMENT
by Peggy Sullivan
LIBRARY PROBLEMS IN SCIENCE AND TECHNOLOGY
by James M. Matarazzo

LIBRARY PROBLEMS IN SCIENCE AND TECHNOLOGY

. . . .

by James M. Matarazzo

R. R. BOWKER COMPANY

New York & London, 1971

Published by R.R. Bowker Co. (A Xerox Company)
1180 Avenue of the Americas, New York, N.Y. 10036

Copyright © 1971 by Xerox Corporation
International Standard Book Number: 0-8352-0486-3 ✓
Library of Congress Catalog Card Number: 70-164033

Printed and bound in the United States of America.

FOR ALICE

CONTENTS

• • • • • • • • • • •

A student organization tries to secure information through the library on a possible manufacturer of chemical biological warfare material whose company recruiter is scheduled to visit the campus.

A board member of a large urban library asks the reason for price increases of scientific periodicals, and requests reconsideration of library budget priorities in a time of community unrest.

A preprofessional in a college library is asked to locate two committee reports identified only by abbreviated titles.

An assistant engineering librarian at an urban university library is asked for standards and specs for home carpeting, and a journal article on Raman scattering.

A student in the process of completing a research project on smoking comes to the high school librarian for guidance because of conflicting research results and complicated statistical problems.

FOREWORD

· · · · · · · · · · ·

It is a paradox that in an age of science, the typical citizen, irrespective of number of school years completed, remains a near-illiterate in science. We have paid dearly in the post-atomic age for a society in which man's capacity to control and alter the environment has outdistanced the ability of an unenlightened citizenry to make sound moral and ethical choices among the alternatives science proffers. Librarians bear a heavy responsibility to master and make available a massive body of specialized scientific literature and information to a variety of clienteles. If the scientifically uninformed citizen is an anomaly in the modern world, the scientifically illiterate librarian is a positive menace.

The library school must provide instruction in the literature of science and technology to groups of students representing highly disparate kinds and levels of academic preparation in science. It is expected to offer courses that are meaningful to students with substantial prior knowledge in basic or applied science, while at the same time providing for those who must be brought, as rapidly as possible, to a basic understanding of the scientific cast of mind and the nature of scientific communication. And all of this must occur in the context of a technical literature that is awesome in its magnitude, and often baffling in its content and modes to neophyte and initiate alike. It is to this thorny cluster of pedagogical problems that James M. Matarazzo's *Library Problems in Science and Technology* addresses itself.

This collection of thirty-five instructional case studies represents the work of an experienced science librarian and a talented, innovative teacher. The problem situations included cut across the range of types and sizes of libraries, and reflect the literature and information requirements of a whole gamut of library users, from the child to the advanced researcher. The approach is at once eclectic and pragmatic, with a consistent focus throughout on the subtle and complex relationship between libraries as information storage and retrieval systems and the varied informational needs of those who use them. The result is a book that should prove eminently useful in both formal and informal teaching-learning situations, while at the same time providing valuable help to the practising librarian who seeks to broaden and update his knowledge of the scientific literature.

Library Problems in Science and Technology is the third volume in Bowker's "Problem-Centered Approaches to Librarianship" series. Like the titles that have preceded it, and those to follow, it is intended to enlarge the body of available case materials for instructional use, as well as to illustrate the value of the case approach in the analysis of professional problems in libraries. As series editor, it is a distinct pleasure for me to have a part in bringing this useful and interesting book to librarians, library educators and library school students.

THOMAS J. GALVIN
SERIES EDITOR

PREFACE

● ● ● ● ● ● ● ● ●

As a consequence of the well-documented decline in the teaching of scientific literature courses in individual subject disciplines at American colleges and universities, a growing instructional burden is placed upon librarians who deal with the technical literature. Because librarians are being called upon increasingly to instruct scientific subject majors individually in the literature, the preparation of library school students who will deal with this literature in professional practice must be both thorough and rigorous. Additionally, the method of instruction employed to teach this subject ought to be one that provides a base upon which the student can build an expanded body of knowledge after he has left the library school. The problem-centered approach to teaching the literature of science and technology can meet those demands if both student and instructor are clear in its objectives and vigorous in their implementation. The best evidence of the success of the case technique is in the reports of former students who find themselves better prepared for the demands of professional employment because of it.

This collection of thirty-five instructional cases is intended primarily for use by students enrolled in graduate programs of library and information science in the study of the scientific and technical literature. These problem cases are, however, also adaptable to workshops, seminars and inservice training programs, for librarians, supportive staff and others concerned with science literature, the communications process in science, or technical reference problems.

The cases included in this volume are based on composites of occurrences drawn from my own experience as a librarian, from the literature, and to a lesser extent, from the experience of others kind enough to share their professional concerns and problems with me. Any relation to persons living or dead, actual places or events is purely coincidental. As a precaution, both place and library names have been taken from the "Index to Foreign Cities" in the premier edition of the *Rand McNally World Atlas* (1943). Similarly, personal names are taken from the "Index to United States Cities" in this same source.

This book includes cases that deal with patents, preprints, technical reports and other special forms peculiar to the scientific literature. In most instances, there is more than one case dealing with a specific form of the literature. There are, as well, a variety of cases centering on scientific reference problems of varying length and complexity. Many of the cases, such as Case 28, "Pugwash et al.," contain both problems in the literature and technical reference questions. Here, the student is asked to locate two conference proceedings, the Pugwash Conference on Science and World Affairs and the Stowe Conference on International Cooperation in Pure and Applied Science. This case, however, also involves a student decision on the value and availability of conference proceedings as a type of scientific literature. It is, of course, possible for the instructor to ask his students to concentrate on the process of locating the two conference proceedings or to question the intrinsic value of conference publications in the larger frameworks of sci-tech literature as a whole. Usually, it will prove more rewarding to leave such choices to the students, who invariably will determine their own priorities in solving the problems posed by the case. Since solutions are presented orally in class, the limitations of individual students' solutions are laid bare before the class. The end result of the individual student's analysis and solution is the collective improvement of the class, and oftentimes, the instructor as well.

The cases in this collection deal not only with problems of collection development, but also with scientific reference questions and sources. For example, the student is challenged to find standards and specifications for household carpeting in Case 4, to locate a translation of a fourth grade science text in Case 31, and to secure biographical information on a widely published physicist in Case 34. These cases, and the others similar to them, are of the fact-finding type, which I have included because I consider them representative of the kinds any librarian should be capable of handling. Some might conclude that the problems are too complex to be considered typical, but I would respond that those able to deal with these questions could only complain of being overprepared—a complaint I, as a teacher, would consider a compliment.

I have not avoided questions of policy as they relate to the literature or to the technical reference problems. Indeed, Cases 1, 10, 15, 30 and others have policy aspects imbedded in them. Although it has not been my intent in constructing these cases to stress policy issues, they are an inevitable consideration in a good many actual reference situations. Class analysis of Case 10, "A Plea for Help," for example, invariably leads to a heated debate among the students as to whether it is appropriate for the librarian in this instance to offer medical information or advice. It was in part my intention to provoke precisely this type of debate, but I remind the reader that this question of policy is only one part of the problem presented.

There are two features of these cases that reflect my own thinking on the instructional case study. The first is the length of the cases. The reader will no doubt find these shorter than most. I have decided, through my experience as a student at Simmons and later as an instructor, that extremely long case studies have a tendency to make the students uncomfortable initially with the method. Consequently, I have attempted to present the problems fully, while at the same time keeping the cases brief.

In addition, this volume includes examples of a variation on the traditional instructional case study, which I have termed the "interested observer case." Case 23, "The *Beaker* Feature," is an example of this, as is Case 25, "A Preprint is not a Publication." In Case 23 the student is allowed to "overhear" a conversation on the future of the scientific periodical where a number of conflicting opinions are advanced. At the end of the case the student, as one interested in the future of such publications, is asked to research the problem, analyze his data and form a defensible position of his own on the subject.

The order in which the cases appear is random, and any application to formal courses should take this into account. In the instruction of the Literature of Science and Technology course at Simmons College it has been my practice to follow an organizational pattern similar to the arrangement of Denis Grogan's *Science and Technology: An Introduction to the Literature* (Clive Bingley, 1970). Other instructors who choose to cover the literature in a different sequence may do so without difficulty while utilizing this collection of cases.

Each case is intended to stand alone as a vehicle for the presentation of one or more problems in a particular setting. Each problem, then, should be resolved within the given constraints enumerated in the case. In general,

I do not think it productive for students to pursue a solution beyond the boundaries defined in the case. Although the order of cases is not sequential, the experiences in research, analysis, decision making and reporting are cumulative over the span of a semester course. Students should be fore-warned that there is no single right answer or correct solution to any of these cases. It is entirely possible for two analysts to produce equally de-fensible solutions that are completely opposed to one another. Case 1, "VX," has provided me with several examples of this phenomenon. In-structors using these cases will hopefully be both vigorous in the pursuit of excellence in student analysis and tolerant when a solution other than the one they might have chosen (or had not thought of) is proposed. If the student can successfully defend and document his analysis before the group, then he has satisfied the major requisite of this method of instruction. Since there are thirty-five cases it should not be necessary for most instructors to repeat any case twice in an academic year. My experience with this method and these cases indicates that it is usually best not to use a given case too frequently, even if it becomes a favorite of the students or the instructor. This, of course, makes the development of new case material an ongoing necessity.

It has been suggested to me that this volume might be more widely used if it were accompanied by an answer book. Those who suggest this evidently have failed to grasp the essentials of the problem-centered ap-proach to library education. In my experience an answer book for this text would have to be serial in nature, as students each semester conceive and defend solutions that have not previously occurred to the author of the problem cases. Herein lies one of the delights of this teaching method.

The preparation of this collection of case studies in the literature of science and technology was begun at the suggestion of Professor Thomas J. Galvin, series editor of the "Problem-Centered Approaches to Librarian-ship" series. Without his advice, experience and editorial skill, this book would not have been possible. I am particularly grateful for the time and interest he has expended on the manuscript as friend, colleague and editor.

All who have worked with the case method at Simmons owe a great deal of thanks to Kenneth R. Shaffer, Director of the School of Library Science, because he has provided the kind of atmosphere and leadership that led to classroom experimentation with the case approach. Because of this atmosphere, I was encouraged to apply the technique to scientific and technical literature.

I wish to acknowledge also the help and suggestions of two Simmons colleagues, Professors Jane Anne Hannigan and A. J. Anderson, and would like to thank as well Miss Maria Cardullo and Mr. Allan Green for discussions of the cases. Additionally, I own a great debt to Miss Karin O'Loughlin for typing this manuscript, and I wish to thank my editors at Bowker, Madeline Miele, Rona Morrow, and Lee Mickle, for their help and advice.

The extensive research done by my former students during the experimental period of case development has made this book better than it would otherwise have been, and I acknowledge their contributions with thanks. To Miss Barbara Moriarity and Mr. Stan Brown, both former students, I extend particular appreciation for permission to include their analyses of Case 35 as examples.

I am grateful as well to the Simmons College Fund for Research for their timely grant which enabled me to complete the research for parts of this manuscript in a more efficient manner.

INTRODUCTION

. . . .

The case method of instruction was introduced experimentally into the graduate program in librarianship at Simmons College in 1951 by the Director of the School of Library Science, Kenneth R. Shaffer. Encouraged by the success of this method in its application to graduate education in fields such as law and business administration, Professor Shaffer initially adapted the case approach for use in the area of library administration, where he has published four case collections, and subsequently in the area of book selection, where he has authored a fifth volume of instructional cases. Basing his work on these experiments, Professor Thomas J. Galvin of Simmons College successfully modified the case technique for use in the beginning reference course. The results of his work appear in two published collections of case studies, *Problems in Reference Service* (Bowker, 1965) and *Current Problems in Reference Service* (Bowker, 1971). Later, Professor Kenneth F. Kister, then also a member of the Simmons faculty, applied the method to the area of social science literature, as exemplified in his *Social Issues and Library Problems* (Bowker, 1968).

To the best of my knowledge, *Library Problems in Science and Technology* represents the first systematic application of the case method of instruction to the scientific literature and related reference problems. For this reason, it seems important to comment briefly on my own goals and objectives for the Literature of Science and Technology course, so that others may understand more fully the rationale governing my choice of a problem-oriented instructional methodology. Other instructors using this collection of cases and the case method may, of course, choose to adopt quite different aims. In any event, this text is designed to facilitate a problem-centered approach to instruction, a major objective of which is to free the student from depending on either the instructor or his lectures.

xxi

The emphasis in a course taught by this method is on developing in the student an ability to produce usable and defensible solutions to specific problems delineated within the boundaries of the case study. It becomes the business of the student to apply those general principles that he judges most germane to the particular problems presented in the cases. The rewards to both teacher and student in implementing and carrying out these objectives are potentially very great. Instructors should not lose sight of the fact that in most instances today's student will very shortly be on his own in professional practice where he must analyze, judge and resolve a variety of complex literature problems that will be placed before him.

During a fifteen-week semester, I have found it both practical and desirable to assign at least fifteen cases for student analysis. Class discussions of the cases and their solutions involve at least one half of the total class period, which comprises one weekly session of 150 minutes during regular semesters. Naturally, the cases are assigned well in advance in order to allow students sufficient time for research. Two involuntary oral presentations are made for each case, prior to opening the problem to general class discussion. The preparation of class note cards facilitates the oral presentations, especially for those required to make the major presentations. These cards are collected for each case, and checked by the instructor in order to judge the level and amount of research done by those not given to extensive participation in class discussion, as well as to review the thinking processes of each of the students. Use of several reference sources is necessary for the solution of most cases. The case method makes it possible to test the individual student's knowledge of sources under conditions for which they were designed to be used—to find answers to specific problems. The artificiality of assigning large groups of technical reference sources to the class for abstract study is avoided with the case method. Actual use of sources in realistic problem citations is stressed instead.

The student's responsibility begins with identification and analysis of the problems contained in the assigned case. His next task is to research the problems and choose a viable solution to the case, usually for oral presentation. On the other hand, it has been my practice to require two written analyses from each student during the semester. The two student solutions appended to case thirty-five are presented as examples of acceptable written analyses. These solutions are comparable in depth of research, but the direction of analysis in each is different. Mr. Brown's analysis stresses the need for higher quality research projects for entry into any high school science fair, and his sources reflect this choice. Miss Moriarty has taken more of an umbrella approach to the questions raised in the case, and her suggested sources indicate this. These solutions are samples, not models. Any student opposed to the concept of science fairs could, and in fact should, make his analysis as persuasive as those of Miss Moriarty and Mr. Brown and prove his point.

The questions at the end of each case are intended to guide the student in developing his solution and to point out obvious issues for his consideration. I have instructed my students to disregard these questions if they choose to concentrate on aspects they judge more significant. In the documentation required for the solutions to these cases, I have given credence to the personal experience of the student as well as interviews (including telephone) and searches of the literature of any and all relevant disciplines.

To some, use of as many as fifteen problem cases in a semester course may appear excessive, but experience in the classroom has proven this untrue. In addition to the many and varied sources consulted and used in the solution of the cases, students enrolled in the Literature of Science and Technology course at Simmons College are referred to a select list of scientific reference sources, and are asked to locate answers to sets of technical reference inquiries. Short presentations are made in class from time to time by the instructor on both the sources and the literature. Students enrolled in this course are also required to prepare an original bibliography, called a "Pathfinder," in a narrow scientific, technical or medical area. The Pathfinder assignment is explained in detail in the Appendix to this volume.

This text lends itself to use by those instructors who choose to divide the scientific and technical literature either by subject (mathematics, physics, translations, etc.) or by type of reference source (dictionaries, yearbooks, biographies, etc.). Both methods have been tested successfully in the classroom here. Again, the instructor will have to decide for himself and his students which pattern of course organization is most comfortable and effective.

Since class size is limited in the School of Library Science at Simmons, I have employed the case approach with sections ranging in enrollment from fourteen to twenty-six students. It has been my general practice to assign the entire class the same case. Of late, I have experimented with assigning two cases simultaneously, with one half of the class simply reading one of the cases while solving the other, and vice versa. This, too, appears to be a satisfactory application of the method. As an alternative to this, an instructor might prefer to deal with the high cost of scientific periodicals in the context of a short lecture, or through assigned readings, in which instance he would probably not assign Case 2, "Moody's Request," but substitute another of the cases dealing with journals, such as Case 32, "A Tightening Budget," or Case 23, "The *Beaker* Feature."

Both the student and the instructor will find "Case Studies and Case Method" by Thomas J. Galvin in the *Encyclopedia of Library and Information Science* (V. 4, pp. 214–219, 1970) of interest in itself and for the selected bibliography on the case method and the instructional case study which is appended to it. Galvin's *Problems in Reference Service* includes two sample analyses and Kister's *Social Issues and Library Problems* includes five sample solutions which can be used to supplement the two sample analyses included in this volume. Professor Galvin's latest collection of case studies, *Current Problems in Reference Service*, contains an expanded bibliography covering the case method, the instructional case study and published case collections.

1.
VX
• • •

"Excuse me. I'm a graduate student and Professor Statford, my advisor, told me to come over here and search my thesis topic in *Chemical Abstracts*. Where are they and how do you use them?"

"Be glad to show you. You mean you've never used *Chemical Abstracts* before this, and you're a graduate student in chemistry?" asked Miss Coomer, subject specialist in the science reference area of the Coin University Library.

"Never had to. Why, is it that difficult to use?"

"No, no, I . . . I was just curious." She and the student were away from the reference desk for about ten minutes, while Miss Coomer explained by demonstration just how one would search a topic in *Chemical Abstracts*. On returning to the reference desk, Miss Coomer thought that the last question was more like the type she'd prefer to be asked. The location of the pencil sharpener, the men's room, or a spare pencil were hardly examples of "reference questions." The more she thought about it, the more she felt her knowledge was being largely wasted. Her training in library science and the subject specialty she had developed were not being used to the fullest extent. Another student came to the reference desk and interrupted her brief daydream with the question, "May I use your phone?"

"I am sorry," began Miss Coomer, delivering her standard reply to this question, "use of these phones is restricted to library personnel. There is a university extension just outside the circulation desk for your use."

"I'm looking for the chemical supply catalogs," said the next patron.

"They're on chemistry reference shelves at the bottom of the first range over there," said Miss Coomer, pointing to the location with her left hand. About three quarters of an hour passed and the student using the chemical catalogs did not seem to be having much success. Miss Coomer was just about to get up and ask if she could help him when he started in her direction.

"It's not in any of those catalogs. I've checked every one of them," said the student.

"I'll call chemistry lab supplies; they have about 200 catalogs. I'm sure what you're looking for will be in one of them."

"Don't bother. I'll just have to locate the information somewhere else."

"Oh, it's no bother. After we find what chemical you're looking for, lab supplies can order it for you right away."

"No. You see I'm doing some research on my own, and I know lab supplies has a rule about not ordering chemicals for noncourse or nonthesis related projects. As a matter of fact, I suspect now that what I'm looking for is relatively new on the market, so that finding it in any of the chemical supply catalogs would be most unlikely. On the other hand, Tirol Chemical would be a likely company for me to check. I'd bet if anyone is producing fluoromethylpincolyloxyphosphine oxide, it's them."

"And it's not listed in their catalog?"

"No, it's not. At least it's not listed in the one I looked at that was published this year. Perhaps *you* could call them."

"If you would be willing to write the chemical name on this sheet of paper along with your name, year, and department, I'd be more than happy to call Tirol and ask them if they manufacture the chemical."

"Oh, that would be swell! My name is Tom Lawton and I'm a grad student in the Chemistry Department. Sometimes, fluoromethylpincolyloxyphosphine oxide is just called Soman, and occasionally it's referred to as VX. I've put it all on this piece of paper for you."

"I'll call right now," said Miss Coomer as she reached for her phone. She first spoke with Mr. Fred Ludlow in the retailing division of Tirol. He was not familiar with the product, but as it was the Coin Library calling, he agreed to transfer the call to his supervisor, Mr. Booth.

"This is Mr. Booth speaking."

"This the library at Coin University calling. I'm trying to locate a compound your company may produce, for one of our graduate students. He needs this chemical for an experiment he's conducting, but we've been unable to find it in any of the chemical supply catalogs, not even yours."

"I'll try to help . . . if I could have the name."

"According to the student, the compound is called fluoromethylpincolyloxyphosphine oxide. He thinks it's sometimes called Soman or VX." Mr. Booth was silent awhile and then responded, "I doubt if it's commercially available or whether anyone, graduate student or graduate scientist, should experiment with it unless very severe controls are placed on the lab. As a matter of fact, it would be very, very dangerous, if not criminal, to use it on a college campus."

"Then you don't manufacture this product?"

"I didn't say that. My division has nothing to do with this chemical. Tirol does have several Department of Defense contracts which, I suppose, puts us in the chemical biological warfare business but not in the production end. The part we play is small, but any part in the manufacture of this compound is extremely unpopular. The company has never publicly admitted it has anything to do with CBW. I'm speaking to you off the record because of the close ties between our company and the university."

"Thank you," said Miss Coomer. "Thank you very much."

Miss Coomer motioned to Tom, who had wandered away from the reference desk, to come back and then asked, "Just why do you want this information?"

"The Graduate Chemists' Student Alliance suspects that Tirol Chemical is involved in the production of CBW weapons. Soman was a lead I was assigned to follow up. Quite frankly, we knew this information would not be readily available to us. On the other hand, a phone call from the library would be respected and honestly answered."

"To what end, Tom?"

"Part of our objection is political and part is humane. Our government has these horrible weapons produced and stockpiled for potential use. The handling, testing, and transportation of CBW weapons is extremely hazardous. No doubt you remember hearing about the animals that were killed in Utah several years ago while the Army was experimenting with these weapons. Well, people have also been killed in the same way. Small countries will more than likely try to produce these weapons, since they are cheap to manufacture. Weapons like VX could become an underdeveloped country's H-bomb, and Tirol Chemical is part of this operation, an operation that could, by accident, become the earth's deadliest polluter. When the Tirol recruiter comes to campus next week, we intend to drive him off campus and out of town. We want to be sure of our ground, so I'm here doing just that. Now, if you know the answer to my question, will you tell me?"

Coin University is a private school with 13,000 students currently enrolled. This center for higher education has never witnessed a violent demonstration in the seventy-six years since its founding. The investment portfolio of the university made substantial gains just prior to the graduation of the son of Hamilton C. Tirol. Mr. Tirol is said to have nearly doubled the endowment of the school by his personal gift of stocks and bonds. In addition, the Tirol Educational Foundation, an independent subsidiary of Tirol Chemical, matched a grant from the federal government and made possible a new science center. The Tirol Science Center provided the university with a first-rate physical plant for the sciences at practically no expense to the school.

Tirol Chemical is one of the largest chemical companies in the nation with offices in several U.S. cities as well as selected foreign countries. This company produces components for many finished products and, thus, few products reach the general public with the Tirol name on them. In the past, the Tirol recruiter has been a welcome guest of the university and the company he represents has been a significant employer of its graduates.

The library at Coin is a central facility, although a small reading room was included in the science center. The central library is divided into subject departments, each staffed by subject specialists. The science reference section, housed on the fifth floor of the library, contains at least one duplicate of each title in the science center reading room as well as a great many more titles. Muriel Coomer has been employed as a subject specialist in the sciences for four years, with particular responsibility for physics and chemistry. In addition to a two-hour daily shift on the reference desk, Miss Coomer is also responsible for book selection in her area and the student staff in her part of the main library. She and two other science subject specialists report to the chief of the Science Division, John Gaffney.

· · · · ·

Decide whether Miss Coomer should give the information she has to the patron. Explain your reasoning. Whether she does or does not give the information, what obligation, if any, does she have to prevent what is planned? Is Miss Coomer at fault for placing the library and the university in a potentially embarrassing position?

Precisely how should Miss Coomer proceed at this point?

2.
Moody's Request

· · · · · · · · · · ·

Galton, with a population in excess of one million, is one of the largest cities in the United States. The last few years in Galton have been marked by increased turmoil among the residents. The last nine months have been scarred by many unpleasant occurrences, including unrest among minority groups, sit-ins by welfare recipients, a teachers' strike, and an extensive fire of unexplained origin at the Galton location of a major branch of the state university. Political analysts concluded that a taxpayers' revolt had the greatest effect on the recent elections when the voters ousted all of the major elected officials and replaced them with members of a reform party. A proposed moratorium on increased spending and the need for a reappraisal of municipal priorities were two of the main issues raised by the successful reform candidate for mayor during the bitterly fought political campaign. As expected, the first official act of the newly elected mayor was to declare a freeze on city budgets at their present level until new studies on the social and economic needs of residents could be completed.

The director of the Galton Public Library has curtailed weekend operations at the main library and several branches, and announced a halt to the hiring of new staff. These measures, along with the natural attrition of staff members who will not be replaced, are expected to be sufficient to forestall any overall increase in the budget of the library. The library has been subjected to unprecedented criticism by several groups from within the community, especially minorities seeking more neighborhood services, and the elderly, who want a greater share of the services of the library directed towards them. The following letter, recently published in the *Galton Tribune*, is indicative of the type of scrutiny the library has had to face for the first time in one hundred and ten years of impressive growth.

To The Editor:

On a recent visit to "our" public library I was stunned to discover some of the ways the city's tax dollars are spent. As President of the

5

Galton Golden Age Association, the GGAA as it is more commonly known, I feel it my duty to expose abuses in the library to the readers of the *Tribune*.

According to price information found in just two periodicals, *Chemical Abstracts* and *Science Citation Index*, these sources cost the library in excess of $4,000 a year. This money could be more profitably spent in the improvement of shut-in service or in programs directed towards the needs of the elderly of Galton.

There are hundreds of these periodicals in this reference area of the library alone, some of which are in foreign languages which must cost even more. You might ask who uses these things? Well, I checked in the hour I was there by making a survey of my own. Of the twenty people in the room, eleven worked in the library, six were students at State, two were tourists and one was lost! Not one soul even approached the periodicals I mentioned earlier.

I left the library in disgust and wrote of my findings to Harold Moody, a member of the Library Board of Trustees, and sent a similar letter to the Editor of the *Tribune*. In the larger frame of reference, I asked myself if this money would not be better spent on food for the poor, housing for the homeless. . . .

Sincerely,
P. T. Spraul
President GGAA

Similar attacks have been made on the library but none more spectacular than the takeover of the bookmobile by black residents of an inner-city neighborhood. The *Tribune* reported the story on page 2 of the evening edition:

FERRY STREET RESIDENTS STEAL A LIBRARY

Several unidentified residents of Ferry Street hijacked the newest Galton Public Library bookmobile this morning as it turned onto the street for a regularly scheduled stop. After ordering the librarian and the driver out of the huge track and driving it to the spot where it usually stops, these same residents carefully removed and secreted the tires.

The bookmobile sits securely atop several large concrete blocks and has been accepted by the community as "their" library. Tables and chairs are on the sidewalk adjacent to the new library as gifts of the residents.

Mr. Robert Sharer, Director of the Galton Public Library, reportedly asked police not to attempt to interfere and requested that the bookmobile be allowed to remain pending a ruling by the Parking Authority.

Contacted by phone, Mr. Sharer expressed the following thoughts on the matter. "Please assure your readers that all possible precautions are being taken to protect public property. The residents of this neighborhood are not going to destroy the bookmobile, but insist that they be allowed to use this facility in lieu of a store front library." When asked about the delay of the store fronts, Mr. Sharer replied, "These neighborhood libraries have been approved by the board of trustees but are presently blocked because of city health, fire, and building regulations." Sharer continued, "The Engineering Department has repeatedly rejected many locations for the store fronts because of the dilapidated condition of the buildings in these areas. Money to construct new branches is not available, as you well know."

A spokesman for the Ferry Street Improvement Association said that Mr. Sharer had visited them and had pointed out the fact that while they had "their" library, many other neighborhoods would be without bookmobile service because of their actions. "We know the librarian is with us and has tried, but trying is not enough." The spokesman went on to say that the residents of Ferry Street would continue to enjoy their library for the rest of the day and that in the morning they intend to return the bookmobile to the authorities.

Only last week Mr. Sharer was interviewed by a representative of the *Tribune* and his philosophy of library service is again condensed for our readers. Sharer would prefer to see the library continue to develop its research capability but not at the expense of needed community service. Pointing to the budgetary problems that have plagued the library in recent years, he explained that many new community programs had been planned and approved but that the money to fund them was not provided by the city.

Defending the large business and science divisions of the library as assets to the students, industries, and residents of Galton, he expressed hope that additional funds could be secured to provide more service in the areas of neighborhood libraries, shut-in service, and the like. Sharer has made it clear on many occasions that the library, containing 900,000 volumes and spending an annual budget of one and one-half million dollars, must maintain standard services and that the new demands of the community must be added to the tasks of the library.

Service on the board of trustees of the Galton Public Library is seen by board members as a civic responsibility and a source of community status. Actions against the public library have placed this community institution, and consequently its board, in the spotlight on more than one occasion in the recent past. Members of the board are not used to this sort of public exposure and are, quite frankly, embarrassed and uncomfortable about the whole affair.

The members of the board include John Fleming, Sherril Professor of Philosophy at the state university; Harold M. Moody, retired president of a management firm in Galton that still bears his name; Gertrude Exmore, heiress to the locally famous Galton Department Store fortune; and F. Perry Aleman, Chairman of the Board of Oneida Electronics. Mr. Moody has received a great deal of mail similar to the letter sent to him by P. T. Spraul and he is determined to clear up several points which are at present of great concern to him. Professor Fleming and Mr. Aleman are by nature more reserved than Mr. Moody but are, nevertheless, as concerned about the problems confronting the library. Mrs. Exmore's behaviour at all board meetings has been the same for the past eleven years. She never speaks once the meeting is under way and always votes the way Professor Fleming does.

Under normal circumstances, the director of the library, in consultation with his department heads, prepares the budget, submits it to the board for what has always amounted to a pro forma approval and presents it to the mayor. The past year in Galton has not been normal, however, and Mr. Sharer anticipates a series of long meetings with the board on the budget. In order to give the board a more dramatic demonstration of the effects of inflation on operating expenses, Mr. Sharer has included 1959 cost figures for each major category of expenditure in his budget proposal, along with estimates for the coming year.

The budget expenditure for periodicals is particularly detailed, since it is divided by subject area. This portion of the budget indicates not only the proposed budget figures by subject area and the 1959 statistics for some categories, but also the number of periodicals to which the library subscribes in each field. The director expects much discussion in this area of the budget by a board that has never examined a library budget in detail and understands very little about the nature of periodical expenditures.

The proposed budget has been in the hands of the board and the mayor for two weeks, and the first board meeting on the budget has just begun. The mayor is not at tonight's meeting because of a death in his immediate family. Mr. Sharer is standing by with several huge folders of data to support his budget request.

MR. MOODY: "The comparison figures are a real help in understanding the budget, Bob. I just had no idea that the library resembles a small business in so many ways. Well—what I want to ask you about are the costs of these science periodicals."

MR. SHARER: "Harold, I sense you're about to comment on the increased cost of these periodicals since 1959. I think that Perry will support me when I say that materials in the science just cost a lot more."

MR. MOODY: "That point is made very clear in the subject breakdown of the periodicals by cost. You haven't always included this data in your budget before, have you?"

MR. SHARER: "No. I would have found it very difficult to present these figures to you were it not for our new agent—subscription agent, that is. The firm provides a list of titles by subject and a complete alphabetical list of our subscriptions as part of their service to our library."

MR. MOODY: "Is this an expensive service?"

MR. SHARER: "No, not really. If the library staff had to order each journal and serial directly from the publisher, the cost in terms of staff time would be greater than the service charge of the subscription agent. Then, too, the city would have to issue separate checks for each title and the cost of this to the city would be even greater. Our service charge for a $35,000 journals budget is approximately 6 percent. This figure varies from year to year and in 1959 we weren't billed for a service charge."

MR. MOODY: "Six percent, and this agency handles 4,000 separate subscriptions for us. How can they afford that? They must get some sort of kickback from the publishers! If they can get it, why not us?"

MR. SHARER: "We pay the agent exactly what we would pay the publisher plus 6 percent for handling the ordering, renewal, and claiming of missing issues."

MR. MOODY: "Still seems awful fishy to me."

MR. ALEMAN: "The increased cost of the scientific titles, the 550 we subscribe to, seems out of proportion to, say, the periodicals in history or the humanities."

MR. SHARER: "That's correct. I have copies of a standard survey done each year for the library field which shows this to be a well established fact. I'll hand these around to you and you will be able to see for youselves."

MR. MOODY: "Why?"

MR. SHARER: "Why,—I must have missed part of your question. I don't understand what you're asking."

MR. MOODY: "Why have the costs of science journals increased three or four times as much as the other kinds of journals? That survey and your excellent statistics say the same thing—this is what has happened. I want to know why they have increased out of proportion to the other kinds of journals!"

MR. SHARER: "I don't know why offhand. But, I'll try to have an answer for yóu at the next meeting."

PROFESSOR FLEMING: "I think we've spent a significant amount of time on one small point. Couldn't we move on to another area?"

MR. MOODY: "In a minute, John. Take *Chemical Abstracts* as an example. In 1959 they charged us about $150 a year. Now they charge in the thousands. Do you think they could have baited us? You know, give it to them cheap for a few years, even if you lose money, and get them used to the source. Then when the hook is caught good and tight, shaft them. In business, we did it all the time."

MR. ALEMAN: "Perhaps the reasons will be available for the next meeting. I'm with John for moving on, but first let me remind all of you of this. My company uses the reference services of the library frequently. In appreciation for the services rendered to my company, the library receives a generous contribution to help finance these services. Many firms that use the public library make similar contributions."

· · · · ·

If you were Mr. Sharer, how would you explain the disproportionate price increases of scientific periodicals to the board?

Can you prove to the board that the 6 percent service charge levied by the subscription agency is not excessive for the periodicals budget of the

Galton Public Library? Could the library subscribe to these periodicals directly with the publishers and save money in the process? If an agency were needed to handle the periodical titles, would competitive bidding be a better way to select a subscription agency?

Based on the information you possess about Galton and its public library, do you feel this library should continue to provide the kinds of scientific periodicals discussed in this case? Can such expenditures of public funds be justified in Galton when the library is unable to find the money needed to support services and facilties being urgently demanded by other segments of the community?

APPENDIX

A selected list of the kinds of chemistry periodicals found in the Science and Technology Department reference room of the Galton Public Library is enumerated below. This list is indicative of the types of periodicals currently received.

Beilstein's *Handbuch der Organischen Chemie*
Chemical Abstracts
Chemical Titles
Chemiches Zentralblatt
Current Contents: Chemical Sciences
Gmelin's *Handbuch der Anorganischen Chemie*

3.
Code Letter—Code Name

. . . .

Highgate State College has a modern central library which is divided into subject areas by floor level. One of these, the engineering reference and research area, located on the seventh floor of the new complex, contains current engineering periodicals, frequently used texts, course reserves, reference books, and indexing and abstracting services that are concerned specifically with engineering subjects. Back files of bound periodicals, and a majority of the monographic works in engineering are shelved with the general collection on the three floors above.

Reference service and collection development for the engineering sciences are the responsibility of three subject specialists, with one of these, the senior specialist, in charge of the overall administration of the area. Subject specialists in this area hold both the master's degree in library science, and an equivalent degree in one of the engineering sciences.

The well-staffed central library is involved in an extensive work-study program with a neighboring graduate library school. Nearly thirty-five employees of the university library participate in this program, which combines full-time work at the library, and part-time study at the library school. The normal time required for a person to complete the program is two years. Job assignments within the library are changed each semester, so as to include work experiences in both technical services and public service areas. During the final period of formal library training which is, in most instances, the final period on the staff of the Highgate Library, the student is given a choice of positions in the library.

Maureen Crosby, a participant in the work-study program, chose the engineering area where she began the program as her final job assignment. Although she does not intend to pursue this subject specialty after graduation, she is interested in the field, and quite fond of both the staff and faculty who work in and use the area.

One afternoon, Miss Crosby was the only staff member on duty in the library, because all three subject librarians were at a faculty club luncheon celebrating the recent birth of the second child of the senior subject specialist. Noticing a familiar face in the library, she asked, "Do you need some help?"

"I've spent almost half an hour already with a young man in the stack area and haven't found a thing."

"Tall, with black glasses, wearing dungarees?"

"That's the one."

"He's a student stacker, and he shouldn't have tried to help you. His instructions are to refer all questions, other than directional, to this desk. I'm Maureen Crosby, and I'm on the reference staff for engineering. Could I help you?"

"Look, I really don't have another half hour to spend here, and besides I asked the boy to help me. He didn't volunteer."

"Perhaps you could just tell me what you're looking for, and we could call you, when we've found it."

"That's better. I need two committee reports: 'ESONE Committee Report 4000e' and 'CAMAC Organization of Multicrate Systems.' The second one is also an ESONE report, dated September 1970."

"No date on the first report?"

"No."

"Could you tell me what these reports relate to?"

"Computers. I've seen ESONE referred to in a computer manufacturer's instruction book and in the literature in the field, but I don't recall what it stands for."

"Could I have your name and telephone extension?"

"Rinard, electrical engineering, extension 9901."

"We'll be able to call you before five o'clock with some information, I'm sure."

When the senior subject specialist, Joseph Minden, returned from lunch, he found Maureen waiting for him. She explained the problem that Professor Rinard had brought to the library, and began to list the steps she had already taken: "I've checked Buttress, *World List of Abbreviations,* and Moser, *Space-Age Acronyms,* and found nothing."

"Moser is mainly in aviation and astronautics," Mr. Minden responded. "Did you check the SLA *Directory of Report Series Codes?*"

"Yes, and *Physics Abstracts,* and *Electrical and Electronics Abstracts,* and *Computer Abstracts.*"

"Rinard, he's in 'double E,' isn't he?"

"He is, but he told me he didn't know what ESONE stands for either. My feeling is that if I can crack the acronym or code, then I have a better chance of tracing the committee report, and locating it."

"What about the title of the second report? Could you search the title?"

"The problem there is that the second report has an acronym, CAMAC, as the first word. I'm caught in a double acronym!"

"Could it be that it's not an acronym? You know like Apollo, the code name that NASA has for the man-on-the-moon project?"

"Then the SLA list wouldn't cover it, because it's a listing of code letters, not code names. What a mess! Well, I'm off to find a directory of code names."

"Don't go yet. Slow down, and think over what you've done so far. Just reflect on it for a few minutes, and see if you've approached the problem in the most efficient way. I might add that ESONE may not be an acronym, a code name, or a letter code. It could be several other things. You try it for a couple of hours, and bring the results of your search to me before four o'clock."

"I'll find it if it kills me!"

● ● ● ● ●

Is it necessary for Miss Crosby to determine the meaning of ESONE and/or CAMAC before she can locate the committee reports for Professor Rinard? If the abbreviations in question are not acronyms, code letters or code names, what are they? Locate the requested committee reports.

4.
Standards and Spex

. . . .

PILAR UNIVERSITY
Office Supplies

To: J. Orlando, Assistant Engineering Librarian
From: H. Wymer, Head, Office Supplies

The legal-size, yellow, lined pads you ordered are available. If you could have a validated request in my office before noon any day, I could have the pads dropped off before the 5 p.m. closing hour of the date of request.

Along with the request for the paper, please send directions on how to use the *ASTM Standards* book for me. I'd appreciate that.

H.W.

Orlando took one last sip of his mid-morning coffee and walked to the office of the engineering librarian. He asked the secretary there to send a request to Supplies for two dozen legal-size pads. Leaving the office for his scheduled time at the reference desk, he settled into his chair and picked up the phone to call Wymer.

ORLANDO: "Henry, this is John Orlando—Engineering Library."

WYMER: "I sent you a memo yesterday afternoon on the special paper. Listen, I'm really sorry about the delay, but the shipping company was in a labor dispute, and we were cut off for almost a month. I hope it didn't inconvenience you, but I had a carton shipped this time."

ORLANDO: "Henry, I called to thank you for letting me know about the paper, not for an explanation. Also, you mentioned the *ASTM Standards* in your note. What do you need the *Standards* for?"

WYMER: "Marge and I are planning to carpet the living room and dining room fairly soon. Like anyone else we'd like to get our money's worth.

15

Every carpet salesman we've talked to says his product's the best."

ORLANDO: "What's all this got to do with the *Standards?*"

WYMER: "One of the faculty said that what I need is probably in the *Standards*. I came over to the library after work a couple of days ago, and a student showed them to me. Now, that set of books is quite complicated, and it sure doesn't work like an encyclopedia, so I couldn't use it. I found out lots of interesting information about different kinds of pipe, nuts, and bolts, but no carpets!"

ORLANDO: "Why not let me help you?"

WYMER: "I don't want to cause you any extra work on my account. I'm sure you have enough to do without my adding to it."

ORLANDO: "Nonsense, I'm here, and that's what I get paid for. You're an authorized user of this library, so I have a responsibility to help you. It's no trouble."

WYMER: "That'd be great . . ."

ORLANDO: "Could you hold on a minute? I see Professor Ellias coming with a slip of paper, and I know he wants some help. I met him in the parking lot this morning and we walked in together. Just stay on the line."

ELLIAS: "Here's the citation—*Spex Speaker,* Volume XII, Number 2, June 1967."

ORLANDO: "No author, just this? Any idea of the subject of the citation?"

ELLIAS: "Raman scattering, I think. I've never heard of or seen the journal myself, but a colleague said to check it."

ORLANDO: "I'll call you as soon as I find out who's got it. I know we don't. You still there, Henry?"

WYMER: "I am. Let me tell you what I've got so far, to save you some work. I called Purchasing because of all the carpeting around the university in the last few years. They told me the company that sells to us doesn't do any residential work. I see you have carpeting in the library."

ORLANDO: "Looks good too, doesn't it? It's been in two years, and is doing just fine."

WYMER: "I told my wife we ought to put down asphalt or vinyl tiles, but she's for the carpet. My own feeling is that tiles are better, and would last a good sight longer."

ORLANDO: "Slow down. You want standards and specs on carpeting for your home?"

WYMER: "Sure, why not? There must be government specs, or an underwriter's laboratory type test that gives you some idea of the grade of what you're buying. The carpet salesmen say 'no,' but I say 'yes'."

ORLANDO: "Now, what about the tile?"

WYMER: "You sure this isn't going to be much trouble? I don't know, banks, hotels, everybody seems to be putting in the carpet, but I would like to win the point with my wife. I just look at that carpeting, and say to myself that tile has got to wear better in the long run."

ORLANDO: "I understand, but I hope you're wrong. There's a lot of dough tied up in the carpet in this library. As a matter of fact, it was installed right over the existing asphalt tile. Let me call you back, two days or so, O.K.?"

WYMER: "Real fine! I appreciate it, and stop in when you're by the office. I'll see if I can have an extra dozen or so of those pads of paper for you."

The engineering library, like the medical library at urban Pilar University, is administratively and financially independent from the central library system. Neither library makes use of centralized processing, largely because of their distance from the main campus. Both derive operating funds from the budgets of the respective schools they serve, and each is under the ultimate control of the school dean. Use of these peripheral libraries by patrons served by the main campus library complex is most infrequent.

The collection of the engineering library, which includes 75,000 bound volumes and current subscriptions to 550 journals, is particularly geared to the technical information needs of its users. Two assistant engineering librarians are responsible for collection development and reference service. For the past five years a special effort has been made to maintain a complete set of the latest *ASTM Standards,* as well as exhaustive sets of standards and specifications from government agencies, professional organizations, and technical societies. Additionally, large numbers of company standards and specifications are received by Pilar Engineering Library from manufacturers throughout the United States.

John Orlando, in his first position after graduation from library school, has been a member of the staff for two years. His casual relationship with Wymer began soon after he arrived at the university, when his initial request for legal-size, yellow pads was rejected because they were not kept in supply. Orlando visited the supply office to ask for them in person. During this initial visit, he discovered that Wymer had graduated from a local high school fourteen years earlier, and had immediately gone to work for the university in the office supplies unit. He had replaced the former head eight years ago, and had grown with the job as the university grew.

•   •   •   •   •

Describe the steps necessary in order to find a library that has the *Spex Speaker* requested by Professor Ellias. Which abstracting and/or indexing services cover this journal?

In Orlando's position, how would you go about locating standards and specifications on residential carpeting for Wymer? Both Wymer and Orlando use the terms "specifications" and "standards" interchangeably. Is this correct? Which sources would provide authoritative information on the relative merits of carpet and tile?

5.
Smoking and Health

· · · · · · · · · · · · ·

"Mrs. Rice, would you help me with the research I've done on my paper on smoking?"

"How can I help?"

"I'm kind of hung up on two or three problems and I'd like some advice. Of course, I want to do the work myself, but I'm in a kind of spot," said the bright member of the junior class at Ridgeway High School.

"Has researching the smoking project given you some problems?" asked Sanchia Rice, Media Specialist at Ridgeway.

"Yeah, the whole thing's a real disaster. I don't know who's right or who's wrong, or what to do next."

"I know you've done a lot of searching here and at Fahler Medical Library on smoking, so let's start with this point first. Are you having a problem with the location of materials?"

"No, not the location of materials. I went to Fahler and the note you wrote for me got me in. A really great guy there helped me, and between our library and the medical library I've accumulated the greatest pile of references ever assembled on smoking. Everyone's been great, but I'm nowhere. I've gathered a lot of data from magazines like the *Southern Medical Journal, Science, Science News* and others. I've sent for and gotten material from the American Cancer Society, Tobacco Institute, Consumer's Union, Public Health Service and so on. I've listened to tapes of news conferences on smoking and looked at the films on smoking in the media center here. When you put it all together, I've got this huge mass of material on smoking, done by reputable scientists, but much of what I've got is in conflict."

"You seemed to have done a very creditable job in gathering your data. Now, if you can evaluate and synthesize it, you should have an excellent term paper for your biology teacher. I hope you found the advice I gave you helpful."

"Oh, I did, and I'm kind of embarrassed to be here again after all the help you've been to me already in the searching of this material. But my paper has a good chance of being a real bomb. For instance, take the best lead I had for proving through laboratory experiments that lung cancer was caused by cigarette smoking. This was a real breakthrough and had never been done before. I first read of the experiment in the *New York Times* where it said that the results were soon to be submitted for publication. Naturally, I wanted to read this and include the evidence in my paper. While I was browsing through a scientific magazine, I read about the experiment again, but this time the results weren't too encouraging. It seems the two scientists, Auerbach and Hammond, who conducted this research, were refused the right to publish their work in either the *New England Journal of Medicine* or the *Journal of the American Medical Association.* Later, the Tobacco Institute used that as evidence to question the validity of the experiment."

"When you first approached me with your problem, you said you were looking for scientific data on smoking and health. Now, are you trying to prove a relationship or disprove it?"

"When I started, I wanted to find the scientific data and form my own decision after reviewing the experiments. Now, I find myself with proof positive on both sides. It doesn't seem to matter *which* side I take. I can provide ample scientific data to either prove or disprove a relationship between smoking and cancer."

"Were you objective in your search?"

"I think I was. Of course, it's a little difficult to be objective about this smoking and health thing. On T.V., you're buried with commercials that say if you smoke you'll get about ten different diseases, never live to retire, and so on. Now, the federal government sponsors some of these ads, but what facts are they based on? Take the nicotine and tar content of cigarettes for example and look at this sequence of events. First, the government does a survey of tar and nicotine content in cigarettes, and then the 'anti-smoke' commercials tell you if you can't quit, at least smoke a low tar and nicotine brand. Then the cigarette manufacturers start advertising low tar and nicotine brands. Now, who's presented any concrete data to show that tar or nicotine in cigarettes has a harmful effect on humans? The literature tells you what you want it to. Scientists are on both sides of the picture and I'm in the middle trying to pick the side I believe. How can that be done?"

"I see that problem very clearly. Now, what else is a problem for you?"

"I hate to do this to you, Mrs. Rice, but the statistics are murder. Each side has statistics, and whenever they want to prove or disprove a point, they survey a sample. If Public Health says 33 percent of a group of smokers had lung cancer, then the Tobacco Institute can prove that 33 percent of a group of nonsmokers had lung cancer as well. Net result, zero. I'm just lost on the results and the statistics. Would it be fair if I asked you to help me?"

The Ridgeway High School Media Center is particularly well financed and well staffed, with a book collection of 12,000 volumes and subscriptions to 180 periodicals. A large and excellent collection of films, both 8mm and 16mm, filmstrips, tapes, and records are available for the use of the students, and the necessary equipment for the proper utilization of these media is at hand in ample quantity.

The media center has a representative collection of material on smoking and health including monographs selected from the *Senior High School Catalog,* as well as documents chosen from the *Monthly Catalog.* The vertical file contains information published by the American Cancer Society, American Heart Association, the Tobacco Institute, and the U.S. Government.

When approached by the student initially, Mrs. Rice had helped him locate items in the card catalog, the vertical file, the *Reader's Guide,* and *Applied Science and Technology Index* as a start. She had suggested he could augment the holdings of the media center by visiting the neighboring Fahler Medical Library, and had supplied an appropriate letter of introduction. Several films, selected from the *Public Health Service Film Catalog, Educators Guide to Free Films,* and the *Index to 16mm Educational Films,* were already in the collection and Mrs. Rice offered to secure any other film the student might want. Mrs. Rice had also supplied Tim with a packet of information from the National Clearinghouse for Smoking and Health.

· · · · ·

Was Mrs. Rice's approach to this problem similar to the one that you would have employed? How should Mrs. Rice proceed from this point? Is it appropriate for her to interpret the data uncovered in the search?

Are the results of research reported by governmental, industrial, and university investigators on smoking in conflict, as Tim suggests? Why were the investigators who established the connection between cancer of the lung and smoking denied the right to publish their results in the two medical journals?

Is Mrs. Rice under any obligation to have a balanced collection on smoking in the Ridgeway Media Center? Explain.

6.
Helpful Sally

· · · · · · · · · ·

The city of Bower has actively supported a large scale urban renewal program which is now in its twentieth year of successful and dynamic operation. The renewal program has two major objectives. The first is to attract back to the city some of the population lost to the suburbs of Bower over the past decade. To accomplish this first aim, high-rise apartment buildings and condominiums have been constructed for all economic levels. The second objective is to make more land available for business and industrial expansion. Firms already established in the city have been encouraged by tax incentives to expand their facilities and new industries have been invited to construct facilities on newly cleared "industrial park" sites. This combination of slum clearance and aggressive development of the cleared land has been very successful, and Bower has been often cited as a model for other cities planning similar programs.

The director of the Bower Public Library has been active in the overall planning of the "new" city, and has developed the collections and services of the library to meet the new demands. The facilities of this large public library are considered an asset to the city in attracting more new industry. In developing the collections of the library to provide more effective service to the business community, the quality of service offered to the citizens of Bower has also been improved.

The feeling at the administrative level of the library is that the Science and Technology Division is the key to an effective relationship with the local business community. This has led to a substantial increase in the budget and staff of this division, which is under the direct supervision of William Ogel, its head for the past ten years. Mr. Ogel, a wholehearted supporter of the development plans for the library, has worked hard to instill a sense of professionalism and specialized expertise in his staff. As a consequence, his staff has learned to respond even to requests for patent and bibliographic searches for the benefit of local firms, services that would have been unheard of in this public library a decade ago.

Late one afternoon, one of the assistant science librarians, Sally Parks, was stationed at the public information desk of the division. Sally was approached by a man who introduced himself as president of the Otas Publishing Company. He told Sally that his firm had just opened a new branch in Bower, and that he was most impressed by the promotional material his company had received about the services of the library. New businesses received such material routinely as part of the development program.

"Is there some aspect of our services you'd like to know more about?" asked Sally.

"Oh, no. First let me introduce myself. I'm Ed Monroe, and as I mentioned earlier, I'm president of OPC. Opening a new office in an unknown area has its problems, and well . . . we'd like to get our company known to the professional community in Bower. Are there any prominent organizations in the city?"

"What kind of organizations—social, scientific, business? Perhaps you should inquire at the Bower Better Business Bureau or the Chamber of Commerce. I can supply you with the names of the people in charge of those organizations and, of course, the phone numbers."

"I intend to make myself known to those organizations, but that's not what I'm after. Do the scientists in this area belong to any particular organization?"

"Well, they belong to most of the national scientific societies—you know the physicists belong to the American Institute of Physics and the American Physical Society, the chemists to the American Chemical Society, and so on. I can't think of any *one* organization here or nationally that most belong to. We often get requests for addresses and spelling of scientists' names from the businesses in the area, and we check the various membership directories. A good many members of these organizations live in this part of the country, but you can best see this yourself by looking at the geographic sections of the indexes over there," said Sally, pointing to several ranges of directories.

"Are all those volumes membership directories?"

"Yes, we have over two hundred directories, ranging in size from the Bower Chapter of Special Libraries Association to the massive AMA directory. We keep only the latest volumes, and I'm in charge of the directory collection, among other things. They're really a difficult set of volumes to manage. Some of them are supplements of journals, some are separately published, and some are just a few pages of journal issue. For example, the Bower SLA membership directory is just a few pages of our August issue."

"You're a member of this SLA organization?"

"Yes."

"Who would belong to such an organization?"

"Oh, the special librarians in the Bower area—librarians in industrial firms, banks, and the like."

"I wonder if I could sit here and look through some of the names in the directories?"

"Of course!"

"You've been most helpful. Could I have your name and the names of the staff members of the library? I want to mail each of you one of our brochures. They're in full color, you know."

Sally gave Mr. Monroe her name and the names of the Science and Technology Division staff members, and for all practical purposes totally forgot about him and his company. Nearly a month had passed since their initial meeting when her memory was refreshed by the appearance of two large envelopes on her desk, both from OPC. She hadn't yet had time to open her envelopes when there was a shriek from Mr. Ogel's secretary. Sally headed to the office to see what had happened.

OPC really had sent everyone in the Science and Technology Division quite a brochure. By most moral standards, but apparently not by legal ones, the material would be judged pornographic in the worst sense of the word. Mr. Ogel and several staff members had gathered round and were attempting to comfort his secretary, who had been the first to open the brochures. As she began to calm down, Sally called Mr. Ogel to one side and explained the episode that led to the receipt of the brochures in the library. After apologizing for an obvious error in judgment, she recalled that Mr. Monroe had spent a great deal of time at the photocopying machine with several directories, including that of the local special libraries organization.

Ogel was understanding but firm in response to what Sally told him. He instructed Sally to take several immediate steps. "First," he said, "I want my name removed from the mailing list, as well as the name of the library. Check with the other staff members who received brochures and see what they want done about their names. Then, by phone or letter inform the Bower SLA Chapter and the other societies, whose membership directories you suspect were used, of what's happened and what they might expect in light of the library's experience. And finally, try to find out if the library has violated the law in any way by allowing Monroe access to the directory collections."

• • • • •

Are Mr. Ogel's instructions reasonable? What problems might Sally Parks encounter in attempting to carry them out? Has she indeed been guilty of one or more errors of professional judgment in providing directory information to Otas Publishing? Is the library responsible for the use to which its directories are put? If so, what regulations would need to be adopted to meet these responsibilities?

7

A Proposed Reorganization

. . . .

The national reputation of Meteghan University derives chiefly from the excellence of its undergraduate and graduate programs in engineering. This far-western center for higher education has twenty-seven academic buildings on its 250-acre campus and an undergraduate enrollment of 7,620. The graduate schools currently enroll 1,500 students pursuing advanced degrees to the doctoral level in the humanities, business management, science, and engineering.

The university libraries are decentralized at eleven different campus locations for all aspects of readers' services. Four are major units—the humanities, science, business, and engineering libraries—and their locations have been planned so as to make them most convenient to the patrons they serve. Seven smaller, more specialized reading rooms reflect a further attempt to place libraries as close as possible to students, faculty and researchers. The engineering library maintains administrative control over two of these reading rooms, one for metallurgy and the other for space sciences. The education and fine arts reading rooms are administered by the head of the humanities library. The science librarian has responsibility for the earth sciences and chemistry reading rooms, with the statistics reading room under the supervision of the business librarian.

The administrative hierarchy of the libraries consists of the director and two associate directors, one for readers' services and the other for technical services. These three top administrators, the heads of the four major libraries, and the heads of departments in technical services (cataloging, acquisitions, and journals) meet monthly to formulate policies for the university library system.

Returning from his usual morning coffee break, Thomas Robinson, Science Librarian at Meteghan, noticed an interoffice envelope on his desk from the Director's Office. Opening it, he saw a covering note from Ruth Varnell, Associate Director for Readers' Services and his immediate supervisor. She asked that he read the enclosed proposal sent to her by the engineering librarian, consider its contents, and make his judgments known, not to the engineering librarian, but to her. The proposal read as follows:

Memorandum

To: Ruth Varnell, Associate Director for Readers' Services
From: C. Harriet Engleberg, Engineering Librarian
Subject: A Proposed Decentralization of the Journals Department

A well-managed collection of journals is a key service to the students, faculty, and research patrons of an engineering library. The unsatisfactory performance of the present centralized system of handling our journals prompts me to propose this reorganization within the libraries. The time has come when we must reevaluate the concept that such a centralized department can serve the needs of the four large libraries and the seven reading rooms. After years of giving it another try, I have found that the system has ceased to perform adequately in my library. The increases in funds and holdings in the past six years have shown journals to be the weak link in the library chain. The engineering library's 980 subscriptions, which constitute a significant percentage of the 9,000 titles presently maintained by the Journals Department, are not and have not received the care and maintenance I feel necessary in order for me to run an efficient library. Below I have again listed our perennial complaints for your consideration:

1. Claiming Procedure. The present system is a duplication of effort and, therefore, a potential delay in getting our missing issues claimed. Under this system we are asked to type on a form the volume, issue, year, and journal title and route it to the Journals Department. They, in turn, type up another claim form and send it to the appropriate agency or publisher.

2. Outstanding Orders. Our unfilled journal orders, some dating back three or more years, are further evidence that this present system does not work. The Journals Department does not follow each order through until the first issue arrives. Once the order is placed by them, no further check is made on the order unless we claim it. Yet, journal acquisition is their responsibility once we have submitted the purchase request. Claiming of missing orders should be their responsibility also. Our patrons look to us to supply them with new journal titles or issues, and when we cannot produce them, it does us little good to explain the

shortcomings of our present system of journal maintenance or acquisition.

3. Duplication of Check-In. Since all issues are sent directly from the publisher to the Journals Department, they check them in first and then route them to us. We check them in here on our visible index file and place them on the current shelf. I fail to see why they check them in when it only causes a further delay between the journal's arrival at the university and its subsequent arrival in our library.

4. Payment and Price Records. These very important bits of information are kept at the Journals Department and they do this part of their job very well. When we call over for this information, we further delay the check-in mechanism. The same staff that keeps these payment records also does the check-in. It is quite obvious that they cannot check in our issues if they are checking prices at the same time.

The handling of all aspects of our journal operation in the engineering library would be more efficient and in the best interest of our patrons. We could do a better job here because of the reduced number of titles we would have to handle. Most important, with a decentralized system, we would not only have the responsibility in this area, *but the control.*

The head of the Journals Department and his three clerical assistants do the best they or anyone could with 9,000 titles to process. The time has come when I realize that I can and will do a better job with this aspect of my library's operation under my control. The result would be better service at a smaller cost in time and money.

C. H. Engleberg

The contents of the proposal were all too familiar to Mr. Robinson, who, on more than one occasion, had made most of the same points. Some differences between the libraries did occur to him as he pondered how he would respond. The science library subscribed to approximately one hundred more titles than the engineering library and seemed to have a higher proportion of foreign titles and translations. Yet, the two libraries were essentially similar in most respects. Both had the same size staff, four professionals and four clerks, both were similar in terms of volumes held and seating, 100,000 volumes and ninety-six seats. As he thought about the problem a little longer, it occurred to him that for the first time he was considering changing the system instead of improving on it.

Technical Services at Meteghan is in the basement of the old central library, now remodeled and renamed the humanities library. Cataloging, monograph acquisition, binding, and journals are all housed in this area. This central technical services arrangement has been moderately satisfactory since it was established eight years ago. The university's physical plant truck picks up and delivers incoming and outgoing mail to technical services and the eleven libraries twice a day. Books that have been cataloged and journals that have been processed are sent to the libraries via this system. The libraries send orders, books to be recataloged, journals to be bound, and the like to technical services. This system generally operates to everyone's satisfaction.

The Journals Department, a former subdivision of the Acquisition Department, was made a departmental unit a year and a half ago. Barry Loray, the head of the department, came to Meteghan University with two years' experience in the journals area in another college library. Much of his initial work at Meteghan was in the area of research, reorganization, and redistribution of work loads among the three clerical assistants. He issued an updated journals list, the first in three years, within six months after his arrival. The list, although well-received and heavily used, made clear many inadequacies in existing journal holdings. Another clerical assistant was assigned to his department, making a total of four, with the prime task of producing a timely updated journals list each year.

Barry Loray has streamlined many of the procedures in his department which enables his staff to process issues and orders in a more organized fashion. Placing 88 percent of the university's journals subscriptions with a nationally known subscription agency has further simplified ordering and billing procedures. The remaining titles are gifts, membership plans, or controlled subscriptions not available through the subscription agency. These must be handled individually by the clerical staff.

Staff, or the lack of it, is the root of the whole problem of journal control as Barry sees it at this point. With more staff, he feels his department would be more effective. His requests for new staff, along with the requests for additional staff in the other libraries, have been tabled because of tight fiscal conditions at the university.

• • • • •

After making a detailed analysis of Miss Engleberg's proposal, how would you respond to it on behalf of the science library, if you were Mr. Robinson? Should he opt to support Miss Engleberg, a detailed reorganization plan for the decentralization of the Journals Department will be needed and should be included in your analysis. Should he elect to remain with the present centralized system, a plan for eliminating the problems posed by Miss Engleberg should be formulated. What benefits to the operation of the science or engineering libraries does the course of action you have selected offer? Under which system in your view would the patrons benefit most?

8

Is Alcohol Addictive?

. . . .

"You look tired," said Toby Lincoln, a preprofessional assistant in the Science-Technology Division of the Kenmore Public Library and a library school student.

"I am," replied Tom Marshall, Assistant Science Librarian.

"Have you seen the paper—the morning paper?"

"Huh?"

"Have you read Professor Seyer's letter in today's paper?"

"I didn't even have time for coffee, never mind the paper. I'm glad you're here. I need a cup of coffee badly. Take the desk for a me for a few minutes. I'll be right back."

"Read the letter first. While you're drinking your coffee, you can plan what we'll need to do." Toby pointed to the "letters to the editor" column in the *Kenmore Post*, where the following appeared:

To the Editor:

The citizens of Kenmore have an opportunity to perform a public service of unparalleled significance for the majority of the residents of our city. I am referring to the referendum petition on liquor licenses soon to be placed before us on the ballot.

Recent research in the fields of genetics and alcoholism has shown that certain ethnic groups—Irish, Scandinavian, French and German—are susceptible to what is called alcohol addiction. For an unknown percentage of these people, alcohol is an addictive substance, similar to drugs, but where everyone is susceptible to drug addiction, not all are susceptible to alcohol. To those who are susceptible (or, in fact, allergic) to alcohol, the intake of even a small amount is very dangerous and often leads to alcoholism in differing stages. As with harmful drugs, willpower cannot always be effective against a physiological craving for alcohol.

No warning is directed to the user of alcoholic beverages that what he or she is drinking could be addictive. The susceptibility to alcohol is transmitted genetically from one generation to the next. The fact that members of these ethnic groups have migrated to America, some of them with the founders of our country, makes no difference at all. The change of location of an individual does not readily effect genetic makeup.

The alcoholic's damage to society, in broken homes and in destroyed careers is not readily calculable. His effect on auto accidents and the resulting deaths directly attributed to driving under the influence of alcohol has reached far beyond the 300,000 mark in the last ten years alone.

The latest U.S. census figures for our city show a simple majority of our citizens are among those most allergic to alcohol. Save a friend, a neighbor, a family—vote "no" on the referendum.

Sincerely,
Wallace B. Seyer
Professor of Nutritional
Biology

"Oh, no!" said Tom. "Where did he get this information?"

"Does it matter?"

"No, but if he'd cited a source, we'd have a lot less work to do. I'm surprised the American Indian is not included in the group that's most susceptible."

"Then you believe him?"

"No, not necessarily, Toby, but it's as good an answer to the problem of alcohol as I've heard. In a way, it makes sense to me. But, that's all beside the point. We'd better get ready. Those phones are never going to stop ringing. I'd better find the boss and explain the letter. You start the search."

"Where?"

Kenmore, a city with over 800,000 residents, located quite near several "dry counties," has granted all types of liquor licenses since the repeal of the Volstead Act. The referendum petition before the voters is the result of a campaign by concerned citizens seeking to repeal the municipal statute that allows the licensing of establishments to serve or sell alcoholic beverages. With city and state elections just three weeks away, tension between groups on both sides of this question is mounting. Various businessmen who depend on liquor licenses for income are particularly apprehensive about the outcome of this referendum election.

Professor Seyer, a respected member of the local academic community, wrote this letter on the day he left for the Guatemalan jungle on a United Nations–sponsored nutritional study. He is expected to be out of the country for at least six months, and for all practical purposes is incommunicado. He has strong feelings on the liquor question and has served as a resource person for many of the anti-alcohol groups.

The Kenmore Public Library's Science and Technology Division, although lacking much by way of monographic and periodical resources, is staffed by able people. The head of the division, an assistant science librarian and a preprofessional assistant are the full-time staff members. The lack of source material is somewhat compensated for by a cooperative arrangement between the medical library of the state university and public library. The public library is the heaviest borrower of materials from the medical library, through local interlibrary loan, and the staff of the public library is free to use the facilities of the medical library.

The medical library, although certainly not one of the largest of its type, is nevertheless far more inclusive in terms of holdings in the pure and applied sciences than the public library. Although the staff of the medical library is not able to provide reference service either to the staff of the public library or to the public at large, a local MEDLARS Search Center is available to all.

The reactions of the ethnic groups singled out in Professor Seyer's letter can be expected to be highly emotional, and the demand for additional information by the pro-liquor groups, the politicians, and the residents of this community can be expected to be quite heavy. Because of past experience with issues that have caused controversy in the community, the staff of the public library routinely prepares itself whenever such questions arise. Several years ago, a letter published in the *Post* about a local sewerage treatment plant sparked a state investigation that lead to the eventual dismissal of two of the principal administrators of the plant. The *Post*, after publication of the letter, asked the public library for information on the plant and on sewerage treatment facilities in general but was told this library had no such information. A bitter editorial that lashed out at the improper functioning of the plant and the resulting pollution of a local river, included a line or two criticizing the library for its notable lack of material on a matter of public interest. Hence, the policy of being prepared to provide information on any questions likely to become a public issue in Kenmore was adopted.

• • • • •

Explain in detail how you would search the literature on alcoholism in order to prepare for questions relating to the Seyer letter. Which sources would you search, and in what order? Can the document or documents on which Professor Seyer's statements are based be located? Are his statements about alcoholism scientifically accurate? What specific kinds of information would be most helpful and appropriate for the Kenmore Public Library to make available to its patrons on this question?

9.
Over Our Heads

· · · · · · · · · · · ·

Constance Shepard had lived in Leon for twenty-two years, raised a family, and then began a new career at age forty-two, when she returned to graduate school and earned a master's degree in library science. Immediately after graduation she applied to the trustees of the Leon Public Library for a part-time position. The board, aware of Mrs. Shepard's credentials, offered her, instead, the directorship of the library, a post vacant for several years, and one that had never been held by a graduate librarian. Mrs. Shepard explained that she still had responsibilities at home and politely, but firmly, asked to be considered for the part-time position for which she had originally applied. The board, with equal tact, offered her the post of librarian on a part-time basis and she accepted.

Five years have passed since Mrs. Shepard became librarian and, although still part-time, she has worked with exceptional vigor at her job. More staff, including a full-time professional to assist her, longer hours of service, and increased use of the library by the residents of this suburban community of 15,000 have all come about during her tenure as librarian. In addition, she has built up the book collection substantially, using the *Public Library Catalog* as a selection guide.

The most difficult task that faced Mrs. Shepard was attracting new users to the library. Some have been attracted by word of mouth and others because they read Mrs. Shepard's column in the weekly newspaper. Still others have heard her speak before various community groups about the resources and services of the library.

Speaking before the Ladies' Lawn Club recently, Mrs. Shepard announced that the library had begun a project to make greater use of the regional library system which it had joined several years earlier. She explained what more active utilization of regional services could mean for the patrons of the Leon Public Library, in terms of expanded reference capability and access to a significantly larger number of books. As was her custom whenever she gave such a talk, Mrs. Shepard included a practical illustration of the reference value of library materials. An avid "do-it-yourselfer" in her own right, Mrs. Shepard chose household stains as her example to the Lawn Club. After enumerating some types of stains she had encountered around her own home on wallpaper, painted surfaces, and the like, she listed a common household ingredient or combination of ingredients that would remove each one. Then she explained that this information was taken from a recent publication available at the public library. She pointed out that material on such subjects as lawn care, paints, wood, disease of trees, handicrafts and hundreds of other subjects was available at the library, often in multiple copy or sometimes even in pamphlet form for free distribution.

Mrs. Shepard arrived at the library the morning following her talk just in time to answer the first telephone call of the day: "Leon Public Library; Mrs. Shepard."

"Mrs. Shepard, this is Mrs. Farrell and I just had to call you about the talk yesterday. I really did enjoy it."

"It was kind of you to call, Mrs. Farrell."

"I've a couple of questions I hope the library would be able to help answer, but I'm rather embarrassed to ask. You see, I've never used the library in the seven years since I moved here."

"As I said yesterday, Mrs. Farrell, we're here to serve as best we can. Don't be embarrassed to ask the questions."

"Well, as you know, last week was graduation week and I had planned a barbecue for my son and the other members of the football squad. I probably don't have to tell you that it rained every day and we couldn't have the barbecue. I want to plan another one before they start school again. The week of September 1 to 6 is the time I would prefer, but I'm not sure it will be possible to have it then."

"What do you mean, Mrs. Farrell?"

"Well, ah—what's the weather like around that week in September? Does it normally rain then?"

"You need a long-range forecast for about three months from now?"

"Right. What is the temperature at about four o'clock in the afternoon—that's when I'd like the barbecue to start. Is it likely to be windy in that part of the day? Is the sun likely to be out?"

"I've got it all down on the pad in front of me," said Mrs. Shepard.

"And the other thing I wanted to ask about has to do with all that rain we had last week, too. I'm fairly sure it does anyway. At least my husband says so. We've developed a musty odor in the basement playroom. I've tried several aerosol cans of fresheners but without much lasting success. Of course, they're quite expensive, too, and I just wondered if your reference books give some household item that would do an effective job?"

"Offhand, I don't know, but I'll find out. Let me call you later."

"Who was that?" asked John Lazore, the full-time professional on the staff, as he entered Mrs. Shepard's office for a first cup of coffee. Mrs. Shepard explained Mrs. Farrell's call and the two questions she had asked.

"Connie, you've flipped. This is not Cal Tech, this is a small-town library, a good one, but a small-town library. Farrell's husband is an electrical engineer and she'll tell him everything we say. If we fail on this, we'll be the laughing stock of the town. Connie, call her back! Tell her she's got us in way over our heads. How can we tell her about the weather in September, when the forecasters on T.V. can't tell us what it's going to be like tomorrow?"

NOTE: The nearest major city to Leon is located twenty-one miles away at latitude 42° 22′N and longitude 71° 02′W.

• • • • •

Is Mr. Lazore correct when he says Mrs. Farrell's questions are beyond the capabilities of the staff of a small public library like this one? How would you proceed at this point if you were in Mrs. Shepard's place? Which sources would you consult in order to give the most accurate answers possible? Would you refer Mrs. Farrell to outside experts on either question? What use of the regional system might you make?

Mrs. Shepard has purchased a great deal of pamphlet material on a variety of subjects, and this material is often given to patrons without charge. Do you consider this a sound policy for a public library like this one? How can the costs of such free distribution be justified?

10.
A Plea for Help

. . . .

Salinas University, located in a large metropolitan area, boasts an excellent reputation in the fields of science and technology. The curriculum is heavily weighted in the pure and applied sciences, although an emerging interest in the humanities, particularly languages and linguistics, has been noted of late. Salinas is a university of considerable distinction, widely known for the excellence of its teaching and research programs. The doctoral and post-doctoral programs offered there in the pure and applied sciences are held in particular esteem, not only nationally but throughout the world.

Supporting both the teaching and research activities of the university are its libraries, with holdings in excess of two and one-half million volumes. The largest of the several libraries on campus is the science library which contains 300,000 volumes, 53,000 technical reports, and 2,200 current serial and journal titles. Its five reference librarians serve the informational needs of the departments of mathematics, chemistry, physics, biology, and earth sciences. Naturally, the science reference collection at Salinas is all that would be expected at one of the foremost technical libraries in the nation.

During the daytime hours of library service, two reference people are needed to handle the rush of inquiries that frequently occurs at the ends of class periods. The reference specialists on desk duty merely push a series of buttons when the need arises and the reserve reference staff emerges from the office area to help.

The morale of the staff throughout the university library system is consistently high, but somehow this esprit de corps is even more apparent in the science library. The science reference personnel have an exceptionally firm grasp of the information sources in their areas of specialization and the patrons of the library draw heavily on this knowledge. The excellent staff and collection associated with the science library are utilized by many neighboring research-oriented companies, which pay substantial annual fees for this privilege. Several of the large firms even employ full or part-time agents who remain in residence in the library to expedite needed literature searches, photocopying, and the like. These company personnel maintain regular contact with their respective organizations through a bank of pay telephones just outside the science library. Other companies that have small special libraries often find that their librarians make two or three trips per week to Salinas to obtain materials in support of research to augment the limited holdings of company libraries.

George Hartwell, a recent library school graduate, considers himself fortunate to be working in the Salinas Science Library. He had first heard of it while a student at an eastern library school and had sought employment at Salinas with the specific hope of an assignment in the science library. Although he does not have extensive academic training in any of the sciences, Hartwell has a strong interest in science. Before coming to Salinas, his only previous working experience was as a library aide while an undergraduate. As soon as he reported for work at the science library, he was assigned a specific subject area, mathematics, and put in charge of a $25,000 plus budget for monographic and serial purchases in this area. He has found his first two months' experience on the reference desk most rewarding. He, like the other reference specialists, is assigned to a four-hour shift at the desk each day. George feels he is gaining in knowledge of the collection and of library procedures as each day passes. The rest of the reference staff have taken him "under their wing" and are guiding his development with expert care. This has been very helpful to Hartwell, especially in light of the single, overriding rule for the reference staff set by the science librarian. Simply put, the rule is that each question asked of the reference staff is to be answered, and answered accurately!

One morning as he entered the library, approximately fifteen minutes before its opening, Hartwell heard the telephone ringing at the reference desk. The caller identified herself as a nurse at Glenwood General Hospital, a hospital located in a residential suburb of greater Salinas. She told him that Dr. Edward Towson of the hospital staff wished to speak with someone in the library about an urgent problem. Doctor Towson then took the phone and presented his problem in a serious, sometimes halting, manner. "I've a man in the emergency room who has just ingested an unknown amount of white acrylic paint. He was spraying a refrigerator at a local factory and foolishly, didn't bother to put on his face mask. His respiration seems quite normal and so does his pulse. His face is red . . . I've already called 'poison control,' but they have no record of a previous case."

Hartwell asked, "Have you a medical library in the hospital?"

"Too small to be of value," said the doctor.

"There aren't any medical schools in the Salinas area, as you well know, but there are several large hospitals. I'll check the data on those to see which are the largest and hope the largest ones can help. Who manufactures the paint?"

"Same question 'poison control' asked. We don't know. The paint comes in fifty-gallon drums and they're unmarked. The factory is checking through a huge batch of invoices to see where this shipment came from, but they've been on it an hour now and no results. That's why I need your help. Can you help?"

· · · · ·

Assuming that the response from "poison control" is valid, indicate precisely what you would do, if you were George Hartwell, remembering that time is of the essence in this matter. What sources would you consult, and in what order? What other resources of the university or of greater Salinas would you try to utilize?

11.
A Problem in Space

· · · · · · · · · · · · ·

Space Sciences is the only academic department at King University that administers and funds its own library. This library, created when the department was established in the early 1960s, is intended primarily for use only by students, faculty, and research staff of the department, and is not part of the general university library system. Books, periodicals, and technical reports circulate to authorized users, but none of this material is allowed off university property. Those not directly connected with the department are permitted to use the library for reference and research, but are not permitted to borrow from the collection.

The book collection of this library, numbering 2,000 volumes, is largely a reference and conference collection, although it includes many of the major texts in space sciences. The seventy journals currently received are retained in unbound form for five years. Although not a NASA Depository, the library numbers many NASA documents among its 26,000 technical reports. Most of these are obtained in microfiche, although an occasional hard copy report is purchased on request.

Peter Grove, the Space Sciences Librarian, is given much latitude in the administration of the library by the chairman of the department, his immediate and only superior. Grove usually brings library problems, especially those related to funding, to George Foster, the administrative officer of the department.

King University has five divisional libraries with combined holdings in excess of one million volumes. The director of libraries was apprehensive about the formation of the space sciences library, fearing that other academic departments would want to follow suit. His fears have proved unfounded, however, because other departments have not been in a position to request the financial support that would be needed for this. But the space sciences library is having problems of its own, as the following conversation between Peter Grove and George Foster indicates.

"Let's face it, I'm out of space! No pun intended, George, but it's time to face the facts. If this department expects to have tables and chairs in the library, I'll need more space."

"I looked at your annual reports for the last couple of years before you came over this morning, Peter. You've been saying the same thing for two years, but you've managed."

"I was able to make space for expansion by discarding the old and duplicate periodicals. This gave me the space I needed for this year. But that's it."

"I can't give you any more room; so you'd better think of another solution. There's just no place to extend the library into and no place to give you for storage. That's the truth."

"I've got a couple of ideas I'd like to try on you. My present procedure is to retain the past five years of each journal title. Now, if I reduced that to two years, I'd gain enough space to get by for a while."

"I don't think the chairman will ever buy it. Your reports confirm that a five year back file is optimal for our department. What else have you got?"

"O.K., George, try this. We'll continue to receive the current journal titles in full size form, and buy the last four years of as many titles as we can on microfilm. This will reduce the space occupied by the journals, which now take up almost two thirds of the library."

"More of those little plastic sheets!"

"No, what you're talking about is microfiche. I propose microfilm, actually 16mm film cartridges. Of course, I'll need a couple of reader-printers for the microfilm . . ."

"Aren't the two we just bought enough?"

"We bought microfiche reader-printers. You can't use microfilm cartridges in a 'fiche' reader."

"What's all that you've got with you now?"

"I went over to the science library and borrowed four bound volumes of *Chemical and Engineering News* and this one cartridge of microfilm," said Grove, holding up the cartridge.

"Don't tell me! That one cartride contains the four bound volumes. You've made your point, but I've been here long enough and know you well enough to suspect that there's a hitch. When you come to this office you normally need money, so I suppose I'll play my role and ask how much you think you need."

"No, not money, George. At this point I want to know what you think about the plan. Just your own opinion on what I've said and what I've shown you."

"Seriously, we know you're running out of room in the library, but I haven't been able to come up with a solution to the problem. The chairman has said to me, and to you, I'm sure, that he's well pleased with the library. The students and the faculty praise it and, as you well know, so do the lab technicians. You've got 200 fans in the department, but I've, unfortunately, got only one budget. So I'll talk on my subject, dollars. We don't have many. I'll tell you what you've heard before, money's tight. So, you prepare a proposal for the two reader-printers and the cost of the cartridges you want to buy, and I'll do the best I can. I'm not promising a thing or committing one red cent. All I'm saying is that I'll read the proposal you submit and do the best I can."

"Atta boy, George! I just wanted to know if you'd be receptive to the package. Let's go to lunch and then I'll head back to the library and begin work on a supplementary proposal for the microfilm journal collection and equipment."

"O.K."

• • • • •

One solution to this case would be to prepare a suitable proposal for Mr. Grove to present to the administrative officer of the department. It should include your choice of the brand of reader-printer to be purchased, the cost, and the reason for its selection. Indicate sources for purchase of microfilms of the journal titles listed in the Appendix, and the cost of these. Your assessment of the impact of microfilm on the users of this library should also be included.

Another possibility would be to offer an alternative solution to the space problem. It should be assumed, however, that simply physical expansion of the library is not feasible at this time.

APPENDIX

King University, Department of Space Sciences Library: List of Journals:

Air Force and Space Digest
American Aviation
AIAA Bulletin
AIAA Journal
AIAA Journal of Spacecraft and Rockets
American Physical Society. Bulletin
Applied Optics
Astronautica Acta
Astronautics and Aeronautics
Astronomical Institute of the Netherlands. Bulletin
Astronomical Journal
Astronomical Society of Austria. Proceedings
Astronomical Society of the Pacific. Leaflets
Astronomical Society of the Pacific. Publications
Astronomy and Astrophysics
Astrophysical Letters
Astrophysics
Astrophysics and Space Sciences
Automation and Remote Control
Aviation Week and Space Technology
British Interplanetary Society. Journal
Celestial Mechanics
Control Engineering
Cosmic
Cosmic Research
Earth and Planetary Science Letters
Electronic Engineer
Electronic Engineering
Electronics
Electronics Letters
Engineering Cybernetics
Experimental Mechanics
Foreign Science Bulletin
Geomagnetism and Aeronomy
Geophysics and Space Dicta Bulletin
IEEE Bulletin
IEEE Computer Group News
IEEE Journal of Quantum Electronics

IEEE Journal of Solid State Circuits
IEEE Proceedings
IEEE Spectrum
IEEE Transactions (All Sections)
Institution of Electronic and Radio Engineers, Proceedings
*International Astronomical Union, Quarterly Bulletin on
      Solar Activity*
International Journal of Control
International Journal of Electronics
Journal of Applied Mechanics
Journal of Applied Physics
Journal of Atmospheric and Terrestrial Physics
Journal of Geophysical Research
Journal of Mathematical Analysis and Applications
Journal of Optimization Theory and Applications
Journal of the Astronautical Sciences
Planetary and Space Science
Royal Astronomical Society Memoirs
Royal Astronomical Society Monthly Notices
Royal Astronomical Society Quarterly Journal
Solar Physics
Solar System Research
Solid State Technology
Soviet Astronomy
Soviet Radiophysics
Soviet Report
Space Aeronautics
Spaceflight
Space Science Reviews

12

Old Science, New Science

. . . .

The original building of the Milford High School complex was completed in 1920, with additions in 1950 and 1965 which doubled the capacity of the school to accommodate its present enrollment of 1,200 students and provided needed laboratory and library facilities. The library is directly accessible during regular class hours, while after school, on Saturdays, and during vacation periods, access is provided by a special street-level entrance. The library seats sixty students with additional spaces for listening and viewing of nonprint materials. As the library is the most recent addition to the complex, its furnishings and lighting are modern and functional. With a collection of 14,000 volumes and subscriptions to 110 periodicals, it is moderately well used by both students and teaching staff.

The librarian, Raymond Kelly, taught in a secondary school before coming to Milford High in his present position seven years ago. Mr. Kelly, a certified school librarian, has one full-time clerk on his staff and a generous complement of student assistants. Students cover the circulation desk at all times when the library is open both during and outside regular school hours and are paid a modest hourly wage for this from school department funds. The Projection Club, a student organization to which Kelly is faculty advisor, handles all the audiovisual equipment both in the library and in the classrooms under his direction. The members of the club are not paid for their work. With much of the daily routine of library operation thus organized, Kelly is able to devote his time and energy to reference service, book selection, and faculty consultation.

Harry Faxon, a science teacher, entered the library and proceeded to the reference collection where he began searching for several items in the encyclopedia collection. Harry looked up a short time later only to find Kelly looking down at him. Kelly asked, "Can I help?"

"Oh, hi, Ray. No, not yet. I want to look around and find out if a few

47

problems that have been reported to me are really problems. I'd like to see you later, if that's all right."

"Sure, but if it's a library problem, you don't have to verify it. I'd be glad to discuss it with you without benefit of a search on your part."

"Maybe that *would* be a better idea. I see we have two or three sets of encyclopedias, but we don't seem to have a science encyclopedia. Now I don't want you to think I'm questioning your professional judgment, but . . ."

"You're not. When I came here, I made the same observation. The chap who was then chairman of the science department said he didn't think we needed one. It was his opinion that the major encyclopedias did a better job, with better people writing the scientific articles, than did the science encyclopedias. Hell, we needed a lot of material then, and still do now, so I used the money we would have spent on a science encyclopedia to build up the book and journal collections. Frankly, I wouldn't object to a science encyclopedia, but I'd hate the teaching staff to think I was wasting money on a source no one wanted, that wouldn't be recommended, and that wouldn't be used. And, I might add, until today, no one's even asked about a scientific encyclopedia."

"I'd disagree with not having one. I think that a general source to provide background would be very helpful, and I think the rest of the science teachers would agree. Which set would you recommend?"

"Let me investigate what's available and report back to you. I'll write a short blurb on each set I locate, and you and the other members of the department can select the one you'd like for purchase."

"All right."

"What are you looking for that requires such a source? Perhaps another reference set would be more useful."

"My kids tell me that the library has very little in the way of current developments in science. For example, do you have anything on cryogenics or cryobiology? Our kids see articles in newspapers and magazines, and bring these topics up in class. We explain what we can, but often we want them to be able to do some independent study and report back to class. Can your library support independent study on topics like cyclamates, DDT, monosodium glutamate, or the dangers of smoking? These are the topics of the day! Next week, next month, there'll be others. I'd like to see us able to support such study. Aren't there science yearbooks or something like that that would help us?"

"The problem is twofold. First, you want standard information that's current. Second, you want a sort of current awareness service that will give students a good basis for independent study. All this in the sciences. Does that sound reasonably correct, Harry?"

"It does. Sounds like a tall order too. I'd like to say I'd help you in some active way, but I can't think of anything to do except present the problem the way the students present it to us. The thought of a custom-designed science information service for our kids entered my mind as I walked to the library, but I guess that was daydreaming. I just doubt that the science teachers would be in a position to help with such a system. However, a system like that would solve some of our problems."

"By the way, I've been thinking about adding a couple of new periodicals to the collection in the science area. The two I have under consideration are *Science* and *Nature.*"

"Fine magazines."

"A little too advanced for high school students?"

"I never underestimate them, Ray. If some of the material or even most of it is a little advanced, it will just stimulate them to dig a little more. If they develop research skills now, those skills should stick."

• • • • •

Would a science encyclopedia satisfy the basic informational needs of the students in this high school as described by Harry Faxon? Which one would you recommend for this library and why?

Are science yearbooks or annuals a possible way to meet the need for current information at Milford High School? Which other sources would be useful in this respect?

Would you consider either *Science* or *Nature* appropriate purchases for this school library? If either of these periodicals were selected for purchase, what other obligation would be incumbent on the librarian?

13.
The Mystery Caller

. . . .

"Science library," answered John Bain to the first ring of the telephone.

"Is this the library at Union University?" asked a frail, female voice.

"This is the science library, ma'am. May I help you?"

"Yes, I hope you will. Could you tell me what's new in chelates?"

"I would if you could be more specific? Exactly what would you like to know about chelates?" The caller repeated her initial request. Each time John would try to narrow the topic or would ask her to be more specific, she would merely repeat the question in a slightly weaker tone. "Would you like current articles on chelates? Is that what you want?"

"Oh, that would be wonderful. Yes, two articles would just be fine."

"Ma'am, I'm going to put you on 'hold' for a moment. It's going to seem like I've hung up, but I haven't," said Bain. "I'll go and check for what you've requested, so please don't hang up." Bain left the reference desk, found the latest issue of *Applied Science and Technology Index,* and searched under the general subject heading "chelates." He readily found two articles and pushed the flashing button on his phone to reestablish contact with his caller. "Hello, are you still there, ma'am?"

"Yes, I am."

John read the authors and titles of the two articles he'd located to his caller. She painstakingly copied the information and thanked him profusely for his efforts.

"Who was that?" asked Susan Allen, the other assistant librarian in the Union State University Science Library.

"I don't know. I think she even made a deliberate effort not to tell me. All she asked and kept asking was 'What's new in chelates?' "

"What's a chelate?"

"I don't know what a chelate is. I'm not a chemist or a metallurgist or whatever you'd have to be to know."

"Then how could you answer the question?"

"Look! I had a woman on the phone, I suspect an elderly woman, who asked me what was new on a particular subject. I sized her up from what conversation we had. I determined she wasn't a technical person, so I used the least technical source I could think of to answer her question. Now, I hope it wasn't the mother of the president of this school, or the wife of some important faculty member, but without further details, and she would give none, I did the best I could."

"Now, don't fly off the handle, I have to tell you something. She called yesterday afternoon, and I didn't know what to do with her. Honest, I thought she was on drugs or something. She kept repeating, 'What's new in chelates?' I reached for a chemical dictionary to find out about chelates, but she hung up on me, saying she'd call back later."

"We give this type of information out all the time. We give out physical constants for compounds we can't even pronounce, or recommend mathematical tables to patrons who are eight levels higher in mathematics than we are. We could never be expected to understand every question we're asked completely. Our job is the location of information and the transmittal of said information to the person or persons searching for it."

The campus of Union State University is located in the heart of a medium-sized city. The university maintains strong ties with the local business/industrial complex. The science library at Union State, heavily used by local industry, is a well-stocked reference and research facility with a significant number of scientific periodical subscriptions and most of the major abstracting and indexing services in the sciences. Three professional librarians, with adequate clerical assistance, handle a significant amount of telephone reference work for outside users, as well as adequately supporting the teaching and research functions of the university in the sciences. Both assistant science librarians devote a large portion of their workday to book selection and reference desk duty.

Three days later the "mystery caller" phoned again, but this time Susan was on desk duty. Susan pressed the "hold" button on her phone and dialed John on the interoffice communication system. When John answered his phone, Susan said, "John, that lady you helped the other day wants to speak to you again. I tried to help her but she insists on speaking to you. She's calling about chelates again and asking the same question."

"Nuts! I'll pick up the call in here. Thanks Susan. Hello, Miss—What did you say your name was?"

"I wonder if you could help me again," said the "mystery caller." "Can you tell me what else is new in chelates?"

"I looked it up for you a few days ago and nothing's happened since then. I mean the source I used won't be coming in to the library again for several weeks. When the new issue arrives, I'll be able to help you again," explained John, a little annoyed that he had been singled out by this woman as her personal reference librarian.

"Oh," said the voice, "that's too bad. I'll call again later."

"Don't bother," said John to himself as he heard her receiver click.

For nearly a month after the first contact with the "mystery caller," she continued to call on a regular basis, about three times a week on the average. Each time she would ask to speak to the "nice young man." Susan found that telling her that John was at lunch or out sick really wasn't a solution, since she would simply call back a few hours later or the next day. Soon the caller realized that Susan normally had the morning shift on the reference desk and that the afternoon was the best time to catch John there. John and Susan called her "the voice," "the mystery lady," and the "mystery caller," and for a while the antics of this woman were a kind of amusing occupational hazard. As the novelty of her calls wore off, however, John became irritated by her requests. "Susan, we've got to get this person off our back! She's beginning to interfere with my normal work routine on the desk."

"I'd be put out too, John, if she were bothering me. What can we do to get rid of her?"

"Let's see the boss and explain the situation to her. Maybe she's got a simple solution."

"Maybe, but why don't we try to get rid of the caller ourselves?"

"That's probably the most efficient way to do it, but I don't believe it's the proper course of action. I think the only thing for us to do is to see Mrs. Gaton and present the problem."

"Well . . ."

"Look, Susan, we don't even know who the caller is. She may be some power on campus or she may be a crank. I think Gaton's the key to the solution. If we approach her in a united way, she has got to see it our way."

"All right John. I'll make the appointment to see Mrs. Gaton for both of us. We'll make it an appointment, so we can get it over once and for all."

Later that afternoon, both assistant science librarians were in the office of the science librarian. "Susan, John—what is the problem?" asked Mrs. Gaton in a most concerned tone.

"We've been bothered by a caller who refuses to identify herself and repeatedly calls the library. She asks for me each time she calls, and she asks the same question each time she calls," explained John.

"How often is repeatedly?" inquired Mrs. Gaton.

"Nearly every day," interrupted Susan. "I often get the calls from her and she asks for John every time."

"Why give her to John when she calls? Why don't you help her? Now, you know I've told both of you not to give your name when answering an inquiry! It only leads to problems of this type."

"She doesn't ask for John by name, she asks for the 'nice young man who helped me before'," explained Susan.

"Perhaps you'd better tell me the whole story."

John explained all the details to Mrs. Gaton. He spoke for nearly fifteen minutes and appeared most concerned and upset about the problem. As had been arranged, Susan supported him fully on all the points he made. "It would appear that we have a real pest on our hands," commented Mrs. Gaton when John had finished his explanation. "I need her name, her address, and her relationship to Union State before I deal with this. Once you get this information for me, I'll handle your problem from this office."

In the two weeks that followed their conversation with Mrs. Gaton, John secured the lady's name, Mrs. John J. Sonan, in exchange for his. Susan got her address under the ruse of sending her an important article on chelates. Susan was the one who finally uncovered her relationship to the university. "Well," said Mrs. Sonan, "my son graduated from the university seven years ago. Now he has a fine job with a research company out west, and he does research on chelates. I help him by sending him references to articles on chelates in my letters. I write him twice a week you know. I want him to do better, so he'll get another promotion."

All the information checked out with the records of the university. Her son had graduated seven years earlier with a B.S. in chemistry, one of seventy-four chemistry majors graduated that year. Mrs. Sonan lived a few miles from the university while her son worked for a company almost two thousand miles away.

• • • • •

PART 1: Answer these questions as if you did not know the identity of the "mystery caller":

If you were in Bain's position when "the voice" called the first time, what would you have done? If you decided to answer her question in the spirit that Bain did, would you have selected *Applied Science and Technology Index* as the most appropriate source? Did John and Susan have a professional obligation to answer the caller's question regardless of the number of times she called? Would you have brought this situation to the attention of Mrs. Gaton as they did and when?

PART II: Consider these questions with full knowledge of the identity of the caller, Mrs. Sonan:

Exactly how should Mrs. Gaton handle Mrs. Sonan's requests for material on chelates? Do you have any suggestions for dealing with Mrs. Sonan's repeated question, short of instructing the staff not to answer her?

14.
The Approval Plan

· · · · · · · · · · · ·

Courtorum today is a busy industrial center with over 14,000 people employed in its many manufacturing operations. Some 900 businesses, of varying sizes, operate within the city limits, with printing equipment and leather goods among the principal products. Recently, a new industrial park has attracted two large electronic firms, which now employ more people than all the other local industries combined.

Historians give this city, located on the south Atlantic coast, a small place in the colonial history of the United States, although not nearly as great as the local historical society would have one believe. The 40,000 residents of Courtorum are not preoccupied with the historical past of their city, but one historical fact that is noteworthy is that the population has neither declined nor increased more than 3 percent since 1900.

In 1910, Albert G. Hopeman donated a building to the city for use as a public library along with a substantial sum of money, the interest income from which is earmarked for development of the book collection. With the Hopeman gift as a model, several other prominent families donated funds for the purchase of library books. So substantial were these and other gifts that it was not until 1942 that the trustees were forced to seek funds from the city for the operation of the Hopeman Library. The original library building, formerly the Hopeman family mansion, still stands in the center of the downtown district. Even to the casual observer it would be readily apparent that it is neither well-designed nor functional for a library operation.

Ernest Michelson was appointed director of the library six months ago, immediately after his graduation from library school. The library trustees made it clear to him at the outset that they were aware of the limitations both of the building and of the 100,000-volume collection. They promised full cooperation in the development of a library program designed to meet the contemporary needs of the community.

Michelson discovered shortly after his arrival that endowment funds were available to make the most urgent physical improvements in the building immediately. These included installation of adequate lighting, a new heating plant, and extensive interior redecoration. He also realized very quickly that the book collection was hopelessly inadequate and badly dated in nearly every area except children's literature. This was compounded by the fact that no weeding had ever been attempted since the library opened. He was given to understand by the trustees that a larger book budget could be obtained through municipal appropriation as quickly as the exact areas of need could be identified. Michelson was especially concerned about the total lack of any modern scientific or technical material in the collection. Because he had had no academic training in the sciences beyond high school, he felt ill-equipped to deal with this problem.

The ten full-time staff members, three of them professionally trained librarians (one in the children's room and two in the cataloging department), were eager to help the new librarian correct the many limitations of the building and the collections. In a series of planning sessions involving most of the staff, priorities were established in terms of physical improvements to the library building and strengthening the collections. While outside contractors progressed with work on the heating plant, lighting, and painting, the library staff began working on weeding programs, the reference collection, and the development of a written statement of book selection policy. At the end of six months, considerable progress had been made in all these areas. The proposed book selection policy was approved by the board. This general statement embodied the principles set forth in the American Library Association's *Freedom to Read Statement* and *The Library Bill of Rights*.

With weeding in the reference area completed, new reference materials could be ordered, processed, and put on the shelves. Mr. Michelson developed a buying list of reference books in science on the basis of titles appearing in *Science Reference Sources* and the *Public Library Catalog*. At about this time, he received a brochure from the Garlin Book Supply House describing an approval-purchase plan for public libraries for monographic works in science and medicine. A few days later, a representative of Garlin telephoned and asked to schedule an appointment to explain the plan. This approval plan was of some interest to the novice librarian, because it promised assistance in book selection in subject areas in which he and his associates at Hopeman felt far from expert.

On the day of the scheduled appointment, the Garlin sales representative arrived at the library and spent a short time checking the shelf list and the book collection in the 500 and 600 Dewey classes. He next sought out the librarian. "Mr. Michelson, I'm Fred Baptist of the Garlin Book Supply House. I guess you're expecting me."

"Please come in and sit down."

"Let me tell you a little about my company to start. Garlin has been in business for ninety-two years. I imagine you've seen our ads in the national library journals. We supply medical and technical books to libraries, colleges and hospitals all over the country. Now, I took the liberty of coming out here early to get a feel for your library. I've spent most of my time examining your book collection, especially in science and technology. If my brief sampling is at all accurate, your library hasn't brought any new 'sci-tech' material for quite a long time."

"That's true. My staff and I have many improvements to work on in the building and the collection. In the collection area, we've concentrated on the reference books as a first project. You probably noticed the new sources in the area."

"A great improvement over the previous collection. Yes, sir, I was here two years ago and Mr. Boulder, I believe, showed me around the library. Is he still here?"

"No, he's retired."

"I've had this territory for fifteen years and I've come to know a great deal about the condition of the libraries in this area, so I know some of the problems you've been facing. What I'd like to do is to present the 'Garlin Approval Plan in Science and Technology' which is especially designed for smaller and medium sized public libraries. Under this plan, we select from the 'Weekly Record' of *Publishers' Weekly* the titles in the sciences of the greatest interest to public libraries. These items are starred by our staff and the list along with the books are shipped to your library once every two weeks. In addition, in each volume you will find a four-part order form with the author and title of the book typed in. Two of these four parts on the form are prelabelled. The first one is labelled 'accept' and the second 're-turn.' If . . ."

"Excuse me, but you said there were four parts to the form in each book you ship. Why are only two of them labelled?"

"The two remaining parts of the form also have the author and title of the volume on them. These are yours to do with as you see fit—another little extra offered by our company to the libraries we do business with. Some of our accounts use the last two sections of the order form as processing forms, temporary shelf lists, or to prepare a list of recent acquisitions."

"I see."

"Let's assume you decide to keep a given book from a shipment we send you. You would merely tear off the first section of order form, the 'accept' form, and return that to us. You would already have the book, so you could begin processing it. On the other hand, you might not want this particular book. In that case, you would tear off the 'return' form and slip in in the book. When you have gone through the entire shipment, you would have two piles; one would be the accept forms and the other, a pile of books with the return sections of the order form in them. The books to be returned you would simply put back into the box and mail to us. The accepted volumes would be on their way to processing and the 'accept' portion of the order form need only be mailed to us in a postage paid envelope we supply."

"Who pays the postage on the books I might return?"

"We do."

"Why should I bother looking through a shipment of books I might not want? I could use *Publishers' Weekly* to order my science books from and not bother with your plan at all."

"First, we offer you a 30 percent discount on each of the books sent to you for consideration. I think you will find this substantially more than is offered anywhere else on this type of technical book. Second, we offer you the opportunity to inspect each book personally prior to the actual selection of the title. This lets you examine the book firsthand and decide its worth. Third, our staff of experts selects the best science and technology titles for your library. One of the biggest problems most librarians have with the whole 'sci-tech' area is knowing what to buy. Let's face it, not all of us are experts in these areas. We're more likely to be expert in reference, history, languages or English, not the sciences. In a nutshell, then, our three features of this plan: a 30 percent discount, personal inspection, and expert advice. Naturally, we would bill you only once a month. This saves you time and money in paying the invoice.

"For twenty-five cents additional on each title you select, we include a set of catalog cards. This option, and the medical books option, are the variables in our plan. Libraries the size of yours will be selecting more in the medical field each year, and we are in a position to include selected medical handbooks, directories, and the like in our shipments."

"Sounds like I'm going to get a great many books in each shipment. How could you possibly know how many books to send me in those bi-weekly shipments?"

"The one item I must have from you is your book budget. We'll submit this to our accounting department and then figure the amount you should be spending in the 'sci-tech' area. If you choose the card and medical books options, we'll figure this in too. So you see, the number of books you'll receive will be proportional to your total budget. We will not bury you with books you can't use or just wouldn't be interested in. That would be bad for us and would probably force you to cancel this service, which you can do at any time."

"My budget is quite small right now. $20,000 is the total, figuring both the endowment income and what's provided by the city."

"We'll use that figure and compute the amount you could best expend in the science area. Could be it would only come out to ten books every two weeks."

"I'd like to discuss your plan with some other librarians and think about the whole thing for awhile."

"May I suggest something. You keep the literature on the plan that I have for you in this packet. I'll have a sample shipment sent to your library within a week, and you can look over the types of material I'd be sending you on a regular basis. Take any one of the books in this sample shipment as a gift from the Garlin Book Supply House and me for letting us present the plan to you."

"Very generous of you, Mr. Baptist. I am not sure I am interested in your plan but I will take advantage of your first shipment."

"Fine, I'm due in this area a week from today. I wonder if we could make an appointment for a similar time?"

"My calendar's free then, but I do hope I've made it perfectly clear to you that I'm not committing the library or myself to the plan at this point."

"That's all right. This is just one plan we have that we thought might interest you. Don't forget we're jobbers as well, and would be glad to handle individual book orders for you. Perhaps we could discuss this aspect when I stop in next week."

• • • • •

Knowing the situation at the Hopeman Public Library, would you accept or reject the Garlin Approval Plan? What is your evaluation of the Plan in general, the advantages claimed for it, and the specific options available under it, in terms of the current needs of this particular library?

15.
Special Export Controls

· · · · · · · · · · · · · · · · ·

The Aeronautics Library at Crysler University provides a wide range of materials and services to augment classroom and laboratory instruction in the department of aeronautical sciences. Located close to the department it serves, the library contains copies of lecture notes, conference proceedings, reserve books, journals, and textbooks in a collection geared particularly to the needs of undergraduate students. The Aeronautical Sciences Librarian, Margaret Fluton, devotes a substantial part of almost every working day to student-generated reference questions ranging in difficulty from simple assistance with the card catalog to bibliographic searches in considerable depth. The students see her both as a friend and as a valued, knowledgeable resource person, not only because of her wide acquaintance with the literature, but also because of her familiarity with the large and often complex Crysler campus.

Members of the departmental faculty and graduate students depend heavily on this library in their research. Mrs. Fluton is often called on to gather large amounts of information quickly when a project is being formulated, as well as to support research while it is underway. Most of the faculty treat her as if she were a teaching colleague and all respect her ability to track through the literature of this field and locate an obscure technical report or conference papers, often from scanty bibliographic information. Constantly on the alert for articles of possible faculty interest, which are promptly photocopied and sent to the appropriate individual, Margaret Fluton also takes careful note of the bibliographic information at the ends of articles. When a work of a member of the department is cited as a reference, the whole article or report is automatically copied and sent to him.

In identifying materials for the collection, she has achieved a high degree of faculty participation in the selection process. Besides scanning major journals in the field, Margaret regularly searches *Scientific and Technical Aerospace Reports, International Aerospace Abstracts,* and *U.S. Govern-*

ment Research and Development Reports for report and journal material of possible interest to students or faculty. An array of new book jackets and photocopies of the covers of recent technical reports are constantly on display in the library, along with the latest conference, symposium, and colloquium information. In these ways, Mrs. Fluton has made the library a focal point of departmental activity and interest.

Mrs. Fluton is neither a graduate librarian, nor, for that matter, a college graduate. Indeed, she is the only member of the university library staff who enjoys full professional status without the usual academic credentials. Twenty years ago, when the department was newly established, she was given responsibility for the library, which was then located in the outer office of the department chairman, a far cry from the ultramodern quarters it now occupies. She is on a first-name basis with all the faculty of the department, some of whom she has known since they were undergraduates. Her popularity with the students is nearly legendary, and members of former classes still drop in to see her, or call her for advice when they have a problem relating to the literature.

This library is a Registered DDC (Defense Documentation Center) User by virtue of the many Department of Defense contracts held by the department. As such, the library is privileged to receive a free copy of any technical report requested in order to support work under contract. The report collection has stabilized at 26,000 items with over 75 percent of these in microfiche. These reports are processed for the library and become part of the collection upon receipt. Many of the full sized reports circulate for the regular two-week loan period just as any other mimeographed item would. A few, such as *Thermophysical Properties of High Temperature Solid Materials,* are kept on reference shelves and are therefore noncirculating.

One afternoon, Mrs. Fluton had a telephone call from Mark Gilbert, the chairman of the Aeronautics Department:

PROFESSOR GILBERT: "Margaret, are we receiving *any* classified technical reports at all, now?"

MRS. FLUTON: "No, none. As you know, the university libraries simply will not handle any classified material."

PROFESSOR GILBERT: "Right! Listen, I've been meaning to bring Professor Berg down to meet you. He's just arrived for a brief stay in this country and he's a personal friend of mine from way back. In two weeks he's due back in Sweden for a conference, and he wants very much to make use of the library while he's here."

MRS. FLUTON: "He was here not ten minutes ago, and he introduced himself to me. I tried to call you, but your line was busy. I gather he's there with you now, so you probably already know the problem."

PROFESSOR GILBERT: "Do you have the report he wants there now?"

MRS. FLUTON: "Yes. But it contains a statement that I'd like to read to you. I'd never noticed it before, but after he left, I found a couple more like it in the stacks. The statement is, 'This document is subject to special export controls and such transmittal to foreign governments or foreign nationals may be made only with prior approvals of Air Force Avionics Laboratory'."

PROFESSOR GILBERT: "Then you know that Professor Berg is a foreign national?"

MRS. FLUTON: "He told me all about himself before I found the report for him. Believe me, I wanted him to have it, but I don't know. He even offered to buy it from me for whatever we paid for it, but I told him if he was in fact allowed to read the report, I'd make him a photocopy. I knew you wouldn't object."

PROFESSOR GILBERT: "No, of course not. Look, could you be persuaded to let *me* take it out of the library, and give it to him, or read it to him? Margaret, I'm on the spot here and I'd like to get off of it as fast as possible."

MRS. FLUTON: "Mark, you are free to do what you think best. I'd hate to see you in trouble with the Air Force over a technical report on which it is clearly stated in three places that you can't show it to a foreign national."

PROFESSOR GILBERT: "Says I can't 'transmit' it. What does *that* mean? Show it, talk about it, or use the information contained in it? What a mess! What's the rest of the data on the report? Someone in the department's probably got a copy and might let him see it. Sweden's always neutral anyway. These damned restrictions on this or that are going to drive us all nuts."

MRS. FLUTON: "AFAL-TR-70-85. Title: *Cost Nondestructive Readout;* in parenthesis, *NDRO,* and then *Aerospace Memory.* First author Bittmann, two t's and two n's. Dated April 1970."

PROFESSOR GILBERT: "Where's AFAL located?"

MRS. FLUTON: "Wright-Patterson Air Force Base."

PROFESSOR GILBERT: "How'd we get that report anyway, if it can't be shown to everyone? You said the library didn't receive any classified material."

MRS. FLUTON: "We requested it through DDC. As a matter of fact, it came in full-sized copy to us. What I'm wondering now is what my responsibilities are for this type of report? Can you hold Professor Berg off at your end while I try to check?"

PROFESSOR GILBERT: "Make it as fast as you can. Find out if there really is a restriction on this report."

• • • • •

What considerations, other than or in addition to governmental regulations, might influence Mrs. Fluton's decision in this case? What agencies or printed sources should she turn to for advice or instructions on how this report is to be handled? Is it her personal responsibility to insure the security of this report? Does Professor Gilbert have the right to show the report to Professor Berg? Explain significance and the rationale behind the statement on technical report AFAL-TR-70-85.

Thermophysical Properties of High Temperature Solid Materials, a set of reference volumes on the Aeronautics Library reference shelves, is a publication of the Macmillan Company. This case states that this set of volumes was acquired by this library as a technical report. How can these contradictory facts be explained?

16.
A New Source

. . . .

"Professor O'Brien, can I help you?" asked Mike Endicott, Assistant Science Librarian at Dawson College.

"Michael, where is the rest of *Science Citation Index?* I found a partial 1964 set, but I can't find any current volumes," shouted Professor O'Brien, Chairman of the Biology Department, angrily.

"I'm afraid that's all we have. It was a sample set sent to us by the publisher several years ago for examination. Do you remember when I spoke to you six months or so ago about the need for this source in our library? I asked at that time if you would help generate interest, so we could get the money in the budget to buy it."

"Six months ago," said O'Brien scratching the back of his neck, "I was right in the middle of that damned book. It's done now and off to the publishers, so I can give you the attention I should have then. By the way, what are you doing here so late, and where are the students?"

"I'm here because each of us works one night a week in order to provide reference service in the evening, and the students are at a movie, a Bogart movie. It really cleaned the library out."

"I know 10:30 at night is probably the wrong time, but I'm in the process of catching up on a lot of unfinished work. At a conference two weeks ago I stopped at the booth of the publisher of this set. Now, I don't know why I stopped. I *never* stop! It's something you learn after a couple of conferences. Anyway I stopped, and I listened for about ten minutes, and I was impressed."

"Impressed with *Science Citation Index?*"

"That's right. Of course, I asked a few colleagues about the *Index.* Some of them had heard of it, some not. It's a strange thing, you know what I mean? If you're a biologist, you know the indexes and the major journals in biology. If you're a biologist, you may even know and respect a source like *Chemical Abstracts.* The people in my field who've used this 'thing' ranted and raved about it. One of the bright young biologists even called it the most important source for a biologist in a library. Now, I have great respect for this young man, but I really don't know enough about the source to use it. What do you think about it?"

"Wow! You've asked one question that's really many questions. Let me begin by saying that *SCI,* that's what we call it in the trade, is not really meant to *replace* any of the standard indexing services. The way I understand it, this source is best used to augment the traditional sources. Unlike the traditional abstracting and indexing sources, *SCI* is interdisciplinary in character. Now, when you stop and think about it, so is much of science. The publishers have selected the 4,000 most important scientific and technical journals and completely indexed those journals."

"Then, *SCI* duplicates the other abstracting and indexing services in the sciences. It's kind of a capsule."

"No, no, definitely not! What it does is very different from what the other sources do. It takes the most important journals, which produce the most important articles, and completely indexes each article. Title, author, location of the author, and all the reference at the end of each article. Then, in the 'Citation' section of the *SCI,* all the cited articles are arranged in alphabetical order by author, and under each cited author, the other authors who cite his articles are listed for the year. Take, for example, the article you wrote in the *Journal of Biological Chemistry* two years ago. In the *Citation Index* there would be an entry for O'Brien, J. L. Under this entry, all the authors that cited your *JBC* article as a reference would be listed."

"I see. But why does it look so darn complicated when you open up any of the volumes?"

"Whether it's complicated or not is rather a relative matter. I'd suggest that *SCI* really is not *complicated,* but just new. You see, it's a citation index. That's new to the sciences, but old to a field like law. If you could sit down with it for half an hour or so, you'd find it really quite simple to use. Look at it another way, Professor O'Brien. Can you remember when you used *Biological Abstracts* for the first time? Now, before you say anything, let me venture the guess that it would probably have taken a similar amount of time."

"Certainly is fascinating. What does the library profession think about this source?"

"I've only been a member of the profession for a year, but I've re-searched this topic fairly well at school, and again when I came here. I'd say they've accepted it, now."

"What do you mean by 'now'?"

"There is sort of an historic sequence of events associated with this source. Offhand, I'd venture to say it wasn't one of the finest hours for the library profession. Let me give you a brief synopsis of the way I see it. When *SCI* first appeared, it was generally palmed off by librarians for minor defects like small print, the noise factor, and a relatively high cost. The next stage I characterize as the testing stage. A few librarians compared it with traditional indexes in an actual search, and concluded it was pretty good. Now, the third and final stage in my analysis of the history of this source is its acceptance stage. I don't mean that librarians have written about *SCI* and accepted it. It's just that the interest of people from outside the library field, like yours tonight, has made it successful. You might say that *SCI* succeeded in spite of librarians!"

"That's a serious charge, isn't it?"

"No, not really. It's a personal opinion. You, yourself, said it looked complicated and you're a scientist. Picture a librarian with the source for the first time, and I'd bet 85 percent of the time you'd see a person in terror. Now, I think that this reaction was normal when the source was new, but I also think the time has come when all libraries our size and larger just have to have it. Oh, that reminds me, *SCI* even made *Winchell,* one of our guides to reference books and sources. So I think it's safe to say it's been accepted by the library world."

"I'm going to try several sample searches in the 1964 set we have in the library. If it's as good as you say it is, I'll help you fight for the funds and solicit support. I doubt you can personally speak to each faculty member or potential user of the *SCI,* so perhaps you could think of a more effective way to reach the potential users."

"I'll try to think of something. Please let me know if I can help you tomorrow when you're trying to use it. I'd be only too glad to."

Dawson College, located in one of the midwestern states, is a coeduca-tional institution with a total enrollment of 6,000 students. All undergradu-ates are required to take at least two science courses. There are 106 under-graduates currently majoring in science. The 500 graduate students working toward master's degrees, the highest degree awarded at Dawson, are fairly evenly divided among the ten departments offering these programs. The

Department of Science has forty graduate students currently enrolled in advanced programs in physics, chemistry, mathematics, or biology. The faculty of this department, which numbers thirty, are engaged in research and publication on a rather small scale. Only two of the science faculty have government contracts, both rather small.

The science library is on the first floor of the science building. This library has a professional staff of three and a clerical staff of three and one-half. The science library with a collection of 30,000 volumes and subscriptions to 1,000 journals, is under the administrative control of the director of libraries, but is a complete separate entity in terms of both technical and public services.

As an interdisciplinary source, *SCI* would have to be purchased from the funds of the four departments served by the library. For over twenty years, each department has received a separate materials budget for the year, and only materials authorized by the appropriate department can be purchased from these specifically earmarked funds. For the past three years, the members of the science departments have refused to share the cost of *SCI* jointly and its high cost prevents purchase from the librarian's discretionary fund, from which other, less expensive, general science periodicals and monographs are purchased each year.

● ● ● ● ●

Would you have presented *SCI* any differently to Professor O'Brien? Did Mike Endicott omit any important aspects of *SCI* in his presentation?

Do you agree with Endicott's analysis of the treatment *SCI* received from the library profession, on the basis of reviews in professional media?

Should the Dawson Science Library subscribe to *SCI?* How could the faculty be persuaded to agree on the purchase of this source?

If the *SCI* were purchased, what collateral obligation would fall on the library and library staff?

17.
Kelsey Cola

. . . .

"Good morning, Professor Kelsey."

"Morning, Miss Swain. I wonder if you could help me with a search? Well, I suppose I mean, would you be willing to do a search for me?"

"I'd be glad to help you in any way I can."

"Let me explain the problem to you and then you can decide whether or not you would be able to help. Please bear in mind that what I am going to tell you will have to be kept in the strictest confidence."

"Certainly."

"I've developed a new soft drink. The principle of my cola-flavored carbonated drink is a relatively simple one. This drink is a mixture of glucose and an aqueous solution of electrolytes. Since it's isotonic, it enters the blood stream about fifteen times faster than water. I'm afraid that the exact chemical composition of the electrolyte solution will have to remain my secret for the time being. I'd like you to search the literature, both patent and scientific, to see what you can find for me on the invention I've developed."

"Sounds rather complicated!"

"I thought it might, so I took the time to write it down for you here," and Professor Kelsey handed Miss Swain a half sheet of graph paper with the same information on it he had given her orally.

"You're planning to call this drink 'Kelsey Cola'."

"Yes, it's right up top on the sheet of paper I just gave you. I mean I'd like to call it Kelsey Cola. Here again, I thought your ability with the literature might prove helpful to me. I'd like to know whether I could use the name for my product. I've never tried to patent anything before so whatever information you locate could only be a help to me."

"I see."

"Now, if the whole problem becomes too much for you to handle, call the Patent Office in Washington and have them do what I've asked you. Charge the phone call and the cost of the search to my laboratory supplies account. I've indicated the number at the bottom of the sheet."

"I was about to ask you about that number. I thought it was your home phone number."

"Well, Miss Swain, do you think you can help me with this problem? I know it's above and beyond your normal duties here, but I have the greatest confidence in your ability. Take the whole two weeks to do it if you need to."

"I'll give it a try, Professor Kelsey."

The Chemistry Library at Bolten University is one of six major departmental collections in science and technology. The libraries of the university contain in excess of 2.5 million volumes. This departmental library contains a 50,000-volume working collection and subscribes to 300 chemical journals. The chemistry reference collection is particularly complete and includes the major abstracting and indexing sources in the field, as well as a generous number of patent reference sources. Because of the significant number of patents generated by the chemical industry, the major series of the Patent Office, including the *Manual of Classification of Patents, Official Gazette,* and the *Trademark Register of the United States,* are in the Chemistry Library. In addition, *Science Citation Index* and *Applied Science and Technology Index* are available to Miss Swain in complete runs.

Shelia Swain, the Chemistry Librarian, does not possess a science degree but is a professionally trained librarian. She has been at her present position two years and has helped Professor Kelsey on a number of occasions in conjunction with the preparation of two of his articles for publication. Up to this point she has used the patent reference sources in her library only for the location of existing patents, when the patent number or inventor has been known. For copies of U.S. patents, the nearby Bolten Public Library is used, as it is a depository for U.S. patents and printed copies of these patents are available there. When Professor Kelsey stopped in the library, Miss Swain was noting the conspicuous absence of patrons in her library, no doubt becuase of the beginning of a two week vacation period at the university.

Professor Kelsey, a fairly frequent user of the library, is a likeable sort of person and a particular favorite of Miss Swain's. When she first came to work at the library, Professor Kelsey took her to coffee one morning and showed her a little of the large Bolten campus. At that time, he was to her a kindly face in a sea of unknown faces. Time has removed the unfamiliarity of both the chemistry department and the university, and Miss Swain has come to know a great number of people at the university.

Kelsey, in his early years at Bolten, published quite heavily, but in the past five years he has gradually reduced his research and publication activities. A full professor at Bolten for the past fifteen years, Kelsey is scheduled for retirement in five years when he reaches age sixty-five.

•   •   •   •   •

If you were Miss Swain, how would you proceed to conduct this search of patent literature? What class and sub-class headings should be searched? Can an existing patent on the product described by Professor Kelsey be located?

Is Kelsey Cola a registered trademark? How should Professor Kelsey proceed if he wishes to use this name for his product?

18.
Liaison
· · · · · ·

Withington College, located in a rural midwestern setting, is earning the reputation of being a fine institution for teaching and research. Nearly 8,000 students attend the college, which offers degrees through the master's level. For some time, departments contemplating future doctoral programs have been active in amassing the faculty, space, and equipment that will be needed to support these programs. The college expects to begin accepting applications for doctoral study in about three years' time. Faculty members, recruited from other more prestigious schools, have been attracted to the college because of the potential excellence of several of its departments. These newer faculty members publish quite heavily in the most respected journals in their fields, and this, in turn, has made the continuing process of faculty recruitment less of a problem. Potential faculty members with impressive credentials now take the opportunity to apply for positions at the college on their own initiative.

The libraries at Withington are not particularly distinguished for a college its size. The majority of the holdings of the library are housed in the central library, a building not fifteen years old, though it looks substantially older. Separate business and science libraries are located near the patrons they serve, but both are under the administrative control of the director of libraries.

The science library contains 44,000 volumes, nearly one quarter of the total holdings of all the libraries at Withington, and subscribes to 910 periodicals. It serves the departments of chemistry, physics, mathematics, biology, and geology. Each of these departments has a library committee to advise the science librarian of the particular needs of students and faculty within the department, as well as to help with an occasional book selection problem.

Actually, the library committees differ substantially from department to department. For instance, the Geology Department's Library Committee has little contact with the library staff, but rather vigorously solicits gifts for the science library from private and government sources. In this way, it has been responsible for adding 3,000 volumes to the library in the past three years, including some long runs of valuable geological periodicals.

On the other hand, the Physics Department's Library Committee historically has been an active, one-man operation that rotates each year to a different faculty member in the department. This year, the Chairman of the Physics Library Committee, and its sole member, is Professor Ido Lamasco. Since his appointment to the committee, Professor Lamasco periodically visits the library and conducts what the staff has come to call "the inspection." Armed with a generous supply of publishers' announcements, he descends upon the card catalog and checks to see that each title he feels his department might want is either in the library or on order. Those titles that do not fall into either category are left on the desk of the librarian as suggested purchases.

Professor Lamasco is an impressive man of forty, with long, unmanageable hair and a strong physique. His mannerisms and temperament tend to intimidate the staff, when he enters the library to present what one staff member terms his "lists of demands for the day." Highly regarded by his colleagues and well respected in the field of physics, Professor Lamasco is very hard working and demands much, not only of the library staff, but of his students and himself.

Lawrence Qulin has been the Assistant Science Librarian for three months, following a two year period as Administrative Assistant to the Director of Libraries at Withington. Very pleased with his transfer to the science library and the substantial increase in salary that accompanied the move, Mr. Qulin, at the direction of the science librarian, functions as a liaison between the library and the library committees. During his first two months on the job, he discovered that most members of the several library committees were away for the summer. It became quite obvious to Mr. Qulin that all library committee activity would be put off until very close to the beginning of the fall semester.

The first faculty member Mr. Qulin could arrange to meet was Professor Lamasco. Their meeting was most cordial, something Mr. Qulin had not expected. They discussed the library in more general terms that Mr. Quilin had anticipated. Toward the end of the meeting, he asked Professor Lamasco specifically how the science library could be more helpful to the Physics Department. Professor Lamasco prefaced his remarks with an explanation of some of the future plans of the Physics Department. Among the items he dwelt on the longest was the Ph.D. program the department was planning to begin in three years.

"Now that I have someone to work with from the library," said Professor Lamasco, "I'd like to move into two areas first. I know you are not in a position to make a firm commitment on behalf of the library, but I hope you'll find what I have to say at least worth listening to. One of the things I miss most in our library is physics preprints. A few years ago, when I taught at Jansen University, the Physics Department there routed hundreds of them around to the faculty. The method of distribution was poor, but the preprints were quite valuable. I wish that the library here could start to collect preprints and display them."

"Then students would have an opportunity to see them too."

"Exactly. Now, don't concern yourself with the problem of having to store large numbers of preprints for extended periods of time. The good ones eventually get published in more formal ways. Six months would be a reasonable length of time for the library to keep preprints. After that, just threw them away."

"There must be hundreds of series of these preprints. Just now I can think of Argonne and Brookhaven National Laboratories, University of Chicago, Stanford University, and so on. Which schools, laboratories, and foreign countries do you think we should start to collect?"

"It's particularly important that preprints be collected because of the college's rural location. I'd suggest we start small and see what develops. Take my area of specialization, particle physics, for an example, and for a possible starting point. I could help you select the centers of high energy physics research."

"Of course, the preprints are free?"

"Oh, yes, but under the present setup, everyone is sending everyone else his preprint, and it's best termed just plain madness. A library location for use, receipt, and organization for preprints is the most economical way to handle the problem. Anti-preprints are another problem, but I believe that's being handled centrally somewhere."

"An anti-preprint?"

"Sure. When a preprint is published, in a journal, for example, it's no longer a preprint. After publication it's called an anti-preprint."

"Let me explain to my boss all that you have suggested to me. I'll investigate preprints and anti-preprints some more for my own enlightenment, and to put myself in a better position to judge the magnitude of the problem. As I recall, you mentioned you had two areas you wanted to discuss."

"Correct. Next, I thought it would be helpful to check our physics periodical titles against a standard list. According to Bradford's Law, a very few journal titles account for the most significant articles. I saw a study somewhere of the physics journal literature that showed that about a hundred physics journals account for almost 90 percent of meaningful articles in the field."

"I was going to say that we have well over a hundred physics journal titles, but I see that's not your point. I'll check the study and let you know what I find out about how we stand."

$$\bullet \quad \bullet \quad \bullet \quad \bullet \quad \bullet$$

Is Lawrence Qulin under any obligation to adhere to the advice of Professor Lamasco? Has Professor Lamasco exceeded his authority as Chairman of the Physics Department's Library Committee by asking that preprints be collected in the Withington Science Library?

Should preprints be collected in this library if their value is as relatively short-term as Professor Lamasco says? Why would preprints be important to the members of this Physics Department? To the students? In Mr. Quilin's place, and after careful study, would you suggest to the Science Librarian that preprints be collected? Why? What problems of acquisition and organization would preprints present?

Can a list of the one hundred most important physics journals be located? What limitations, if any, does a list of this kind have as a selection tool for the Withington Science Library?

19.
Of Science
Reference Sources

. . . .

Small talk is not allowed in the science library. Not that Ben Carabine, Science Librarian at Afton College, has ever had to ask anyone to keep quiet. Over the years, the students have set the tone of the library and, as a group, they demand orderly behavior from all who use it. Ben has been at his post for twenty-two years and the serious atmosphere in the library was there before he arrived. Even an occasional non-science major uses this library, when he has some serious studying to do. The same paneled rectangular room has been the location of this library for thirty years. During this period the collection has grown to 39,000 volumes and the seating capacity has been reduced to fifty-one.

Ben's staff comprises only two full-time assistants; one, his secretary, and the other an evening supervisor. The only professional on the staff, Ben orders new materials, handles reference questions, computes the budget and acts as faculty liaison between the teaching departments and the science library. The technical services department of the main library orders and catalogs science material, while part-time student aides handle bindery preparation, circulation, and stacking the science library's 350 current journal subscriptions.

Ben is at Afton because he chooses to be there and not because other positions are not offered him, both within and outside the system. Over the years he has refused many substantial offers from other colleges and universities. Recently, nationally prominent Meredith University invited him to be their science librarian. Although he refuses the jobs offered to him, he is normally asked to suggest other likely candidates for these positions, and, more often than not, he has an appropriate name to suggest. The present science librarian at Meredith, for example, owes his job to Ben who recommended him strongly for the post. Many people at Afton speculate about why Ben stays in his present position. Some say he is just plain content, whole others conclude he is a dedicated alumnus serving his alma mater as best he can. His performance on the job, given the budgetary and space limitations of the science library, has been most satisfactory.

New science faculty meet Ben as a regular part of their orientation to Afton at the insistence of the department chairmen. Ben offers new faculty special consideration while they are getting settled and invites them to submit for purchase by the library lists of books needed for teaching and/or personal research. At Ben's suggestion, each department chairman has available a special fund for the immediate library needs of new faculty. New faculty are always pleased to hear of the library's arrangements for the loan of materials and for the use of the Meredith Science Library, especially after observing the rather meager collection in the Afton Science Library. The mere mention of a connection with Meredith University brings broad smiles to the faces of new science faculty, because it is well known that Meredith has unusually strong resources in the sciences. The science library at Meredith is considered one of the top fifteen in the whole country and is probably closer to the top than to the bottom of that list.

The usual routine of the day was broken one afternoon when a secretary from the physics department delivered a note to Ben from one of the department's newest faculty members. The note read as follows:

From the Desk of Herman Canter

Dear Mr. Carabine:

I would like to request the removal of the *International Critical Tables* from your reference shelves. These tables were published over a half century ago and represent work that is substantially older than the date of publication indicated. For this reason I feel one of my students (or any student for that matter) would make a serious error by using this source for needed physical constants. The registrar of the college informs me that we have 427 undergraduate science majors and ten graduate students in the physics department, the only science department offering a graduate program. I am unalterably opposed to any of these students using this source.

Sincerely,
H. L. Canter
Assistant Professor

Ben read the note and went to the reference section to check the title page of the tables. Rapidly gathering his initial thoughts, Ben composed the following memo and sent it to Professor Canter:

Afton College
Science Library

Dear Professor Canter:

Thank you for your memo on the *International Critical Tables.* Based on your suggestion, I have labelled the spine of each volume of these tables with their publication date. Anyone using them will immediately be aware of the date of publication. However, this is only an initial step. Tonight, at the Science Librarians' Round Table, I will confer with Charles Arco, my counterpart at the Meredith University Science Library, about the *International Critical Tables.*

I'll phone you before the end of the week with my final decision. I appreciate your interest in the library and regardless of the outcome of this problem, I hope your interest in the library will continue. I am eager to cooperate with you, but my final judgment must be based on what is best for the library as a whole.

Sincerely,
Ben Carabine
Science Librarian

That night at the meeting, Ben sat next to Charles Arco and their conversation eventually came around to the *International Critical Tables.*

"As you well know," said Arco, "we don't have a reference section, but rather a series of reference areas based on subject matter. The *Tables* are not only on my physics reference shelves, but on physics reference shelves in every science library I've ever been in."

"Did you realize they're fifty years old?"

"Is that right? Personally, I find them simple to use and I used them a great deal when I handled reference questions. I still see my staff using them, and as a matter of fact, I remember we recently had the index volume rebound. I really put the pressure on bindery to get that volume back, and they did it too! But, why did you ask?" Ben explained the note he had received from Professor Canter and the steps he had taken as an interim measure.

"That's a coincidence," said Arco, "I had a run-in with Dr. Foskett over a physics reference source last week."

"Didn't he get the Nobel Prize a few years back?" asked Ben.

"That's the one."

"What happened?"

"Foskett ducked into the library last Monday and pulled off a volume of the *Handbuch der Physik*. He tried to charge the volume out at the circulation desk but the clerk referred him to one of my reference librarians, who explained the noncirculating status of reference books in our library. Five minutes later he was in my office pacing back and forth, raving about his publisher's deadline. He sat down and told me point blank his time was too valuable to spend all day reading this volume in the library! He insisted he be allowed to take the volume out!"

"Well, what happened?"

"I gave it a little thought. I didn't want to set a precedent you know—if faculty can take out reference books, so can students. So I compromised. I called Bea Shepard in the Humanities Library and told her Foskett was in the library and wanted to take out one of my reference books. I explained I was loaning it to her library for a few days but that Foskett had the volume. Foskett got up, thanked me and left."

"Foskett's in the Humanities Department, right?" asked Ben. Arco nodded in the affirmative. "I suppose it was a face-saving gesture on your part, but why have the rule if a little prestige and writing a couple of books can change the rule?"

"Well, Ben, he had a good reason, and we had an older edition of the *Handbuch* in the stacks should anyone have needed the volume he had out. Besides, Foskett agreed to keep it in his office. I suppose he would have called the provost, and the provost would have called the director of libraries, and so on, if I had said no. I just saved a lot of time this way."

"Perhaps you did—any word on a new edition of the *Critical Tables?*"

"I'll check it in the morning," said Arco as he jotted a note to himself. "Fifty years is quite an unhealthy age for any reference source."

Next morning at the Afton Science Library, Ben found another message from Professor Canter which read as follows:

From the Desk of Herman Canter

Dear Mr. Carabine:

I used the library card you provided me with to gain entrance to the Meredith Science Library last night. I am well aware of the fact that they have the *Critical Tables* on their reference shelves, but my opinion about keeping them on our reference area has not changed. Putting labels on the spines of volumes may be a step in the right direction, but it's not necessarily the answer.

May I suggest you and I write to NBS and urge that a revised edition be put out. Perhaps, your friend at Meredith would join us in requesting a new edition. His participation would certainly make our case a lot stronger.

Further, the National Bureau of Standards must realize the value of the source. I am surprised librarians all over the country haven't been active in getting them to come out with a newer source that has the scope, ease of use, and authority that characterize the old *Critical Tables*.

Sincerely,
H. L. Canter
Assistant Professor

· · · · ·

Comment on the manner in which Ben Carabine has handled Professor Canter's request thus far. Would you have handled it differently? What should Ben do next? Is there a newer edition of the *International Critical Tables* and/or another source that could be called its successor? Are Professor Canter's opinions about the *International Critical Tables* ones which you would subscribe to? Should these tables be removed from the reference shelves at the Afton Science Library?

Would you have handled Dr. Foskett's request differently? Should certain faculty members or others at Meredith University be exempt from the circulation rules of reference books under any circumstances? How can situations like the Foskett encounter be avoided?

APPENDIX

A list of physics reference sources on the reference shelves of the Afton Science Library:

AIP Checklist of Books for an Undergraduate Physics Library. 1963
American Institute of Physics Handbook. 1963
Gray, H. J. *Dictionary of Physics.* 1958
De Vries, L. *Dictionary of Pure and Applied Physics.* 1963–1964. 2V
Handbook of Chemistry and Physics. Latest edition.
Handbuch der Physick. 1955+
Landolt, H. H. *Landolt-Bornstein Zahlenwerte und Funktionen aus
      Naturwissenschaften und Technik.* Neue Serie. 1961+
Nuclear Data. Section A, 1965+; Section B, 1966+
Physics Abstracts. V.1, 1898+
Whitford, R. H. *Physics Literature: A Reference Manual.* 1969

20.
To Know a Fly

. . . .

Sheldon Technological Institute, an independent, privately endowed college of science and technology, offers both undergraduate and graduate courses. The student body of 2,400, equally divided between undergraduate and graduate, is drawn from all geographical areas of the United States as well as from several foreign countries. The undergraduate division awards Bachelor of Science and the Bachelor of Engineering degrees, while the graduate division offers degrees at both the master's and doctoral levels in the fields of aeronautical, electrical, mechanical, and nuclear engineering, as well as in mathematics, metallurgy, physics, and chemistry. The faculty of the Institute numbers 125, with a research staff of nearly equal size. Both faculty and research staff are heavily engaged in a wide range of research projects, some highly theoretical and others with a more practical bent. The administration strongly encourages faculty research.

The Sheldon Library is a modern structure which contains 60,000 volumes, plus 14,000 unclassified technical reports and 850 current subscriptions, chiefly to technical journals. This central library facility is intended to meet the informational needs of students, faculty, and researchers and is the only library on the urban campus. Through a triparte cooperative agreement, the research collections at the neighboring Belder University Libraries and the Belder Public Library augment Sheldon's holdings. The resources of the Medical Library of Belder University are particularly welcome, since medicine is not heavily represented in the Sheldon collection.

The staff of the Sheldon Library numbers twenty, including seven professionals. Three new professional staff positions were created a year and a half ago and filled by recent library school graduates. The new staff members—Bill Shoals, Serials Librarian, Elaine Hugham, Assistant Cataloger, and Frank Lorentz, Assistant Reference Specialist—first met at an informal reception held to welcome them to the library. Their friendship was instantaneous and has developed into a fine professional working relationship. For over a year, these three youngest and newest members of the staff have regularly eaten lunch together at the Institute cafeteria. Occasionally, discussions at lunch center on aspects of their work at the library, and they have learned much from one another about their respective positions from these exchanges.

Today's luncheon conversation began in a work-related vein, probably because Elaine was late in arriving.

"Frank, I sent you a note on the periodical, *Welding Design & Fabrication,* you called about yesterday. As I recall, it was for a faculty member?"

"Right. Is it free?"

"I think it will be for him. It's a 'controlled circulation' journal and all he'll have to do is fill out a form. The Serials Librarian at B.U. sent me a photocopy of the form, and I sent it to you with the note."

"Controlled circulation?"

"I didn't know what it meant either till this morning. As I understand it, you establish yourself as a qualified recipient by filling out a form. If you are engaged in any aspect of scientific research or management, they send you the journal free."

"Would you or I qualify?"

"I don't know, but I'll find out."

"How can the publisher afford to give the periodical away?"

"Oh, it's not free to everyone. If you're not a qualified user, you pay the regular subscription charge."

"They give it away to some and charge others? What would happen if the library wanted a copy? Would we pay or would we qualify for a free subscription?"

"Frank, I don't know. But I'll find out the full story as soon as I can. On the photocopy I sent you there is one other statement I haven't come across before. I can't remember the exact wording, but it implies that some organization audits the circulation. It doesn't say why it's audited or what it means if the circulation of a periodical is audited."

"I was thinking it might be a good item for the library, even if only for the browsing collection."

"Technical Services to the rescue, again! You guys up front would crumble without us! You don't look like you appreciate the dig. As a matter of fact, you look like you've got a problem."

"Aah, I had a tough reference question just before lunch. I worked on it for thirty minutes and came up with zero."

"Let's hear it. If it's got you stumped, it must be a classic. Come on, you've had tough questions before. What's so special about this one?"

"No, not at lunch, especially not today. What are you eating—the special?"

"It's American chop suey and it tastes just fine. The question, Frank."

"Professor Winthrop's secretary called and asked about a fly."

"The common, household variety bug?"

"That's the one. She asked me for information on the fly as it relates to its ability to take off and land on the ceiling."

"You're making this up!"

"No! Listen! Professor Winthrop left a note for her to call the library and check it out. She read some of what he wrote to her over the phone about the three schools of thought on the matter."

"You can't be serious!"

"Oh—yes. Picture a fly on the ceiling. Now, think about how it gets off the ceiling and into the air again."

"Wait a minute. I'll do better than that, I'll watch the one up there—gone!—it happened too fast. I don't know how it's done. What department is Winthrop in?"

"Aeronautical engineering."

"Oh, no. I know submarines look like whales for a reason, but I just can't picture aircraft looking like a fly! Tell me about the three schools of thought."

"School A: The fly drops from the ceiling, does a slow half roll (head to toe) and goes on its merry way. School B: The fly drops from the ceiling, does a half loop and goes on its merry way. School C: The fly drops from the ceiling for a brief period of free flight, finds itself moving in the desired direction, applies the power and goes on its merry way."

"I'm for School B."

"Schools B and C, according to Winthrop's note, are a little more random than nature would normally allow."

"What's the problem?"

"Where do you look to answer a question like that? We've got a superior reference collection, the major abstracts and indexes in every subject field taught here. If you put the holdings of the three libraries in the cooperative together, you come up with over 1,200,000 volumes. I have to find out about a fly in a sea of information! I'm just plain stumped. Maybe I've got a mental block on this one, I don't know; and he's at a conference and wants the information phoned to him."

"Here comes Elaine, let's tell her the problem." Elaine sat down at the lunch table and listened to the whole episode. Her reply took both Bill and Frank by surprise, and seemed quite out of character for her.

"The more I hear about public services, the more I'm convinced that my decision to work in a technical services area was a sound one. I, personally, would object to conducting a search for such a trival matter. What's more, I wonder if Professor Winthrop would even pursue the question if it weren't for the free reference service provided by the library. That man probably can't even use the library. Why? Because people like you, Frank, are there to spoon-feed the information to him.

"Part of any investigation he's conducting is the location of data. Why should you spend hours dragging up material for him? Four or five hours of his time in the library would do him a world of good. Besides, the subject's disgusting."

· · · · ·

How would you respond to Elaine's statement? Could the desired information be related to Professor Winthrop's research or teaching at Sheldon?

Indicate how you would proceed, if you were Frank, to locate the information about the fly. Which sources would you use? Would you expect these sources to be in the Sheldon collection?

Would a librarian at Sheldon be qualified to receive *Welding Design & Fabrication* on a free basis? Do you consider this title an appropriate addition to the collection of technical periodicals at Sheldon? To the browsing collection? What significance, if any, does the audit statement of a controlled periodical have for the Sheldon Libraries? For the faculty member who originally inquired about the publication?

21.
A Proposed User Study

· · · · · · · · · · · · · · · · · · ·

Dan Richards, one of four Assistant Science Librarians at Payson University, had an idea he wanted to discuss with Henry Dagham, the Science Librarian. Dan made an appointment to meet with Mr. Dagham in his office just to insure that they would have enough time to consider the idea fully with the fewest possible interruptions. Mr. Dagham's willingness to listen to the ideas of his younger staff members was one of the major attractions of working in the science library. While at his job slightly more than one year, Dan had proposed many ideas that he hoped would make a good library better. Some of Dan's ideas and the ideas of other staff members were tried while some were rejected, but always after careful consideration by all concerned.

Less than a month ago, for example, Dan had asked for and received permission to experiment with a new method of arranging the cumulative indexes to *Chemical Abstracts*. By observing and helping patrons when they used this set, he noticed they always had a particular subject, author, or formula for which they were searching. Why not arrange the indexes in the way they were used instead of the way they were published? Four shelves on an enormous abstracting table were clearly labelled "subjects," "authors," "ring," and "patent." The cumulative indexes were placed on the appropriate shelves, each volume labelled with a tag and numbered in ascending order, the first volume of the subject cumulations being tagged "S1," the next "S2," and so on. Author, patent, and ring cumulations were arranged in a similar order. This method eliminated the disorder of the cumulative indexes and facilitated searching. Reshelving the index cumulations became a simple matter of being able to count and, as such, saved the stack boys many hours of frustration. The arrangement was accepted by faculty and students as a real contribution; and they took time to make their opinions known. Mr. Dagham and Dan decided to arrange the second set of *Chemical Abstracts* indexes in similar fashion. This set had been held in reserve in the traditional organizational scheme of the indexes as a precautionary measure.

Having been encouraged by the success of his idea, Dan was now prepared to approach Mr. Dagham with a more ambitious suggestion. As he reached Dagham's office, making last minute notes on his yellow, lined pad, he was noticed by Mr. Dagham, who was in his outer office speaking to a student.

"Good morning, Dan. Go right in and sit down, I'll be with you in a minute."

"Morning, Mr. Dagham."

"O.K., tell me what's on your mind," said Mr. Dagham, smiling, as he noticed the note pad in Dan's lap.

"The way I see it we've got a good traditional library. Good staff, reasonable salaries, a fine collection . . ."

"Is this a speech? We've been this route before, and you should know that I'm always interested in your ideas. Now, skip the formal introduction and get to the heart of the matter."

"No, no speech, but this is not just an idea, it's more of a concept . . . I mean it's a real departure from . . . No, I'll tell you the truth. I thought it over and came to the conclusion that I'd better write out the introduction, so you wouldn't think that I was a smart aleck. Not that you ever have, but you don't know what I'm going to say."

"O.K., the floor is yours, Mr. Richards."

"We provide seats, reserve books, reference service, and maintain a healthy stream of new material coming into the library. Now, I'm wondering if this is all we should be providing?"

"I probably shouldn't have interrupted you, because now I'm lost. What did you have in mind?"

"I'm not sure and that's why I'm sure something's missing. We see very few faculty and darn few graduate students in the science library. The undergraduates have to come because of the reserve book system, but, I'd bet we'd lose them too, if it weren't for the reserves."

"Then, you're worried about the number of patrons?"

"Partially. A few faculty and graduate students do use the library, but the vast majority of both these groups must satisfy their informational needs elsewhere."

"We can't force potential patrons of the library to use it. Our job is to have what they want when they come."

"That's what I mean by 'traditional.' As big as we are and as well as we're funded, we don't draw the troops to the library. The question is why?"

"You feel we are missing something, and that's the reason we don't see a large segment of the science people, whom you feel should be using the library?"

"Let's find out what our patrons want and expect from us, and then compare the results with what we give them."

"How?"

"A user survey of all our potential patrons."

"What information would we or could we expect to get?"

"Two kinds. The first would enable us to strengthen, if needed, our traditional types of service. The second would enable us to expand into a gray area."

"Gray area?"

"Where do the science faculty and their students get their information? If the basic assumption I used earlier is correct, then we really service the information needs of a few. If the others don't come here for what they need, where do they go? To a colleague? To another library? Or, to their own files? Perhaps they use the telephone or the mails, but they must use something if they are not using us."

"Dan, you've given me food for thought as usual, and I appreciate your taking the time to do it. Now, let's see if I can add to your thoughts. Who's done this sort of survey before, and what were the results? Were the results ever applied to a library situation or has the work in this area been just on the theoretical level? Would the results be beneficial to the whole library system or just to our library, which services the needs of five departments in the pure sciences? My point in raising these questions is twofold and is not an attempt to put 'cold water' on your ideas. In the first place, maybe our problem has been solved by someone else. Now, if this is the case, our efforts would be just a duplicate of a previous survey. We try to help our patrons avoid costly errors like this one, and we should treat ourselves in the same manner. Second, a project such as the one you've proposed would probably require money and maybe some staff. I need to know the scope of previous surveys in order to measure the benefits we'd accrue from such a venture. This information would also help in writing a proposal for staff and funds should we decide we need to do so. What do you think?"

"I think I should have anticipated your questions and been in a position to answer them. I didn't, so it's obvious that I have some searching to do. If you don't mind, I'll get right to it."

Payson University is a privately endowed institution located in one of the major industrial cities of the United States. The university has a good national reputation, but the schools of management and science are thought to be particularly distinguished. With a total enrollment of 15,000, including 4,500 graduate students, the university is divided into twelve schools. Each school is responsible for graduate and undergraduate courses, and each has a separate teaching faculty.

The school of science provides courses in nearly all fields of the pure sciences and offers advanced degrees to the doctoral level in mathematics, biology, chemistry, and physics. Many of its 450 faculty members are leading authorities in their areas of specialization, but teach both graduate and undergraduate courses. The undergraduate science courses are taught largely by the lecture method with graduate assistants in charge of laboratory periods. Most graduate science courses are seminar courses,' and the faculty direct all of the laboratory work of the 750 students enrolled in graduate science programs.

The library system developed alongside the school organization of the university. Each school has a major library facility associated with it, and several of the schools have additional smaller departmental libraries that are not part of the university library system. The administration of the libraries is centralized in the office of the director, who, in concert with three associate directors, handles most questions of general library policy. Once a month, the heads of the twelve school libraries and the top library administrators meet to consider major policy issues. Technical services are totally centralized and all procurement, cataloging, and binding handled through this division; on the other hand, public services are totally decentralized through the twelve school libraries.

The science library is located in the heart of the science facilities and is the only library serving the school of science. This library has 150,000 volumes, receives 2,000 current journals and purchases 9,000 technical reports yearly. By adding 3,500 new titles to the book collection each year and discarding almost as many old titles, the library has sufficent growth space for at least five more years. Almost 1,000 people enter the science library every weekday during the school year.

Four subject specialists are each responsible for collection development in at least two areas, and two hours of reference duty. Under Mr. Dagham's direction, collection development means responsibility for discarding as well as purchasing, and each staff member has the competence to handle both tasks. None of the subject specialists has a science background, but each has become "expert" in the particular areas assigned to him.

The reference area is moderately busy, largely because the reserve book collection is adjacent to it. There are a total of 2,700 volumes currently on reserve for both undergraduate and graduate courses. Most of the questions asked of the reference staff are directional, with occasional exceptions. Normally, one reference librarian can handle both the phone and desk for a two-hour shift. During the evening and weekend hours of operation, an experienced clerical employee handles the reference desk.

Those faculty members who do use the library use it regularly, requiring little assistance from the librarians, but fewer than 10 percent of the science faculty use the library with any regularity. Those who use the library are aware of its fine collection and able staff. Even the nonuser faculty regularly send suggestions for book or journal purchases. As a matter of fact the largest number of suggested purchases come from faculty in nonuser groups. These faculty members seem content to know the library is there with its staff and collections.

Dan's latest suggestion was prompted by his experience on the reference desk and from general observation of the 250-seat library in operation. Most of his time on the reference desk is spent helping students locate reserve books or helping secretaries check page references. By his observation, the students use the library as a study hall in most instances and not for the research capability of the collection. He feels the library can and should be doing more for the faculty and the students of this university.

• • • • •

Evaluate Mr. Dagham's suggestions regarding the proposed user study. Does a user study already exist which would negate the need for the proposed Payson study? How would you account for the failure of science faculty and students to use this library to maximum advantage? How can the library better adapt itself to meet the informational needs of the scientific community at Payson?

How should Dan proceed in planning the proposed user study? What factors should be considered in planning such a study? How would you estimate the costs of a user study for the Payson Science Library? What values would such a study have that might serve to justify its anticipated costs?

22.
No Agriculture

· · · · · · · · · · ·

"Are you in charge?"

"I am. I'm the head librarian and my name is Lillian Dickerson. May I help you?"

"Explain something! I've put in several requests for a book I'd like to see in the library. The first of those forms I filled in was dropped in the box over two months ago. Now the people at the desk out there tell me what I wanted hasn't even been ordered. To the best of my knowledge, what I've requested isn't the least bit expensive and . . ."

"You're the . . . please sit down, Mr. . . ."

"Parry, Jack Parry."

"Please, Mr. Parry, I think I can explain everything if you would just sit down a minute."

"All right."

"I have the forms on my desk, the ones you filled out. I've just finished checking our registration file for the letter 'B' in an effort to locate you. Now, the whole thing is our fault, and I hope you will believe me when I tell you that I am sorry it happened."

"What's happened? From what I know nothing's happened, and that's why I'm here."

"When the printer supplied us with the new 'suggested book purchase cards,' the forms you filled out, we discovered he had left off the 'please print' label. We sent most of the forms back and have manually annotated about a month's supply just for our current needs. I don't know exactly how to say this to you, Mr. Parry, so I'll just be frank—we could not read a single word you wrote on the forms."

"May I see them? I guess I did scribble."

"Without your name we couldn't call you to ask the title of the book or journal you'd requested. Your last name does lend itself to many variations just by changing the first letter, which we weren't sure of, and by some cler-

90

ical error the forms you used lacked the 'please print' annotation."

"Well, I guess I caused my own problem, and I should be the one to apologize."

"We suspect the first word is 'agriculture' but the staff and I didn't think it could . . . What I mean is, this city doesn't have any agriculture associated with it, past or present."

"What I meant to suggest was the *Agricultural Yearbook.*"

"Oh, yes. I've heard of that series, but have had little, if any, contact with the source. However, we have reference books in the library to help us evaluate such volumes."

"Perhaps, I could make up some of the trouble I've caused by saving you some time, as I am quite familiar with this set of yearbooks. The *Yearbook* doesn't contain much farming or agricultural material any more. In my estimation, the more recent editions would have broad appeal, and the contents of these volumes would be applicable to many aspects of society. When I worked for the Department of Agriculture, I had access to all these publications, but made little use of them. Now I have the time, because I've recently retired and moved to Rodes Point."

"I'll keep your information in mind when I'm conducting my search on this series. Now that I have what I need, I'll give your request my prompt, personal attention."

"Let me add that many of the other publications of the Agriculture Department would prove very valuable for the people of our city."

"I'll look into those publications as well and again I must thank you for your very helpful suggestions. One more thing, Mr. Parry, I wonder if you would mind telling me why you've suggested this source for purchase?"

"I have a tree on my property that I suspect is one of the oldest living trees in North America. My limited studies lead me to suspect that one of the *Agricultural Yearbooks* contains the information I need to prove this fact."

"Our staff can work on the problem for you, if you'd like. I suspect from my days as a children's librarian that the sequoias are the oldest, but that was many years ago."

"Perhaps I've phrased my question poorly. Surely, the giant redwoods of our Pacific coast are among the oldest living trees, but I know my tree is not a redwood. Two, maybe three, years ago I saw a newspaper article that reported some research on the subject, but I'll be darned if I can remember what city I was in or exactly what year I saw the article. The gist of it was that for many years the redwoods were considered not only the oldest trees but the oldest living things in the world. Then, it goes on to tell of this other tree that was much, much older."

"I see. You want just the name of this tree?"

"That would help, but a picture of the tree and its leaves would also help me in making a positive identification."

"Expect to hear from us shortly about the book you've suggested and the information you've asked for."

"Thank you. Oh—before you go I want to tell you that I think the new branch libraries are a darn good solution to a real problem. I know the children in my neighborhood just love theirs."

"Excuse me."

"Come on in, Terry, Mr. Parry was just leaving," said Mrs. Dickerson to Terry Vincent, one of the library's high school student assistants. "What's the matter?"

"The editor of the *Gazette* is on the phone, and he wants to know exactly how rare a perfect bridge hand is. And the lady who reported it is on another line and wants to know the same thing!"

"Sounds like an epidemic. Do you have any specifics?"

"Mrs. Sunning's bridge group had it happen to them less than an hour ago, and they called the paper. The paper has a reporter and a photographer there now. The editor wants to know exactly how rare it is so he can send it in to the wire services. Both of them seem quite excited about the whole thing."

"This is going to be one of those busy afternoons."

"Oh—one more thing. The man from the paper said he doesn't want the opinion of one of those 'bridge experts' on the perfect bridge hand. He wants some 'real scientific data' on the subject."

For almost fifty years the Rodes Point Public Library served the residents of a city of 150,000 from a single library facility in the downtown area. With parking a significant problem and the decay of housing in the central city area, the patronage of the library had decreased steadily over the past decade. Proposals for a bond issue, which would have allowed for construction of badly needed branch libraries, have been soundly defeated by the voters each time they appeared on the ballot.

A career librarian with twenty years' experience in public library work, although director of this library for only a short time, Mrs. Dickerson had been very active in soliciting community support for the proposed branches.

With the need for branch libraries readily acknowledged by the users of the library, the city government, and the board of trustees, but little hope of finding the necessary funds, Mrs. Dickerson devised, fought for, and won approval of a rather unusual solution to the problem. With trustee authorization, she worked with the mayor to secure the release of three older fire stations which were vacant because of a recent centralization of fire protection in the city. At the time these fire stations were constructed, fire fighting apparatus was horse dawn and more limited in range and speed than the present motor driven equipment.

The new branches were ideally located. Two were in the residential sections of the city, and all three were adapted inexpensively for library use, while retaining much of the outward appearance of fire stations—something the children of the neighborhoods found very appealing. The taxpayers of the city and particularly the residents of the immediate neighborhoods were pleased at the results, the former by the fiscal aspects, and the area residents by the relative quiet that is associated with a library operation during the sleeping hours.

The city has two small private colleges and a fairly sizeable industrial area. In the core area of the city, dilapidated tenements and modern high rise apartment buildings are but a few blocks from one another. Outside the downtown section of this southwestern community, one and two family housing units predominate.

The residents of Rodes Point are largely middle class, and for the most part take a great deal of pride in the appearance of their property. Although no official statistics are kept, many homeowners in the residential sections of the city have small flower or vegetable gardens, but, as Mrs. Dickerson noted, no one would ever characterize the city as agricultural. Problems with taxes, drug abuse, and the youth of the community occupy much of the thoughts of the residents and much space in the city's daily newspaper, the *Gazette*.

The book collection of the Rodes Point Public Library, numbering 148,000 volumes, was previously housed in toto in the main library. In the two months since the new branches opened, some 15,000 volumes have been transferred to them, mainly children's books and light fiction. The reference collection at the main library is below average in size and quality, and would be more characteristic of a much smaller public library. Prospects for more funds for materials are not good because of recent increases in the library budget for personnel to staff the branch libraries.

Mrs. Dickerson is one of only three professionals on the staff. The children's librarian and a cataloger are the other two members of the staff with library training. At present, the children's librarian is dividing her time among the new branches in a supervisory role. Although almost no original cataloging is done at the library, the professionally trained cataloger is in charge of the small clerical staff that handles acquisition, cataloging, journals, and binding. In addition, there are twenty-five other full-time library employees, some with college degrees, three of whom are in charge of the branches, which are open from 10 to 6 Tuesday through Saturday.

Reference and circulation are normally handled by the clerical staff at the main library, and another clerk has been recently assigned to the children's room to cover for the absent children's librarian. The main library has more generous hours than do the branches, being open until 10 p.m. each evening, which is generous indeed when one considers that municipal support for this library is slightly less than $1.60 per capita.

Last year 4,000 volumes were added to the collection and periodical holdings increased by three titles to 250 subscriptions. As the main library reached shelf capacity several years ago and an addition or new central building were not possible, the new branches had first priority for Mrs. Dickerson. She now plans a vigorous campaign to increase the budget and professional staff of this obviously very poorly supported library.

• • • • •

If you were in Mrs. Dickerson's place, how would you handle the problems raised in this case? Would this library be likely to have the sources necessary to answer the bridge question? How would the answer best be located?

Would the *Agricultural Yearbook* be an appropriate purchase for this library? What other publication of the Department of Agriculture, if any, might be considered for purchase? Identify and locate a picture of the oldest living tree and its leaves. Would the library be likely to have the sources needed to answer the questions raised by Mr. Parry?

23

The Beaker *Feature*

· · · · · · · · · · · · ·

The Beaker, a publication of the Graduate Science Student Association at Askin College, appears four times during each college year. An interdisciplinary journal, *The Beaker* normally carries feature articles as well as scientific news of particular interest to its readers. Major articles are written either by students or by faculty members with an occasional invited article by a leading scientist from outside the college.

At a recent editorial planning session, Julian Gauley, Assistant Editor of *The Beaker* and a graduate student in the Psychology Department, was discussing a proposed feature article for a forthcoming issue with Simon Snow, Assistant Professor of Chemistry and faculty advisor to *The Beaker.*

GAULEY: "I've done a brief outline of this as a possibility for the June issue, but I'd like your opinion on the whole question. I begin with a statement Price made in 1963 in *Little Science, Big Science:*

> Even in the seventeenth century, we must not forget that the motivating purpose of the *Philosophical Transaction of the Royal Society* and the *Journal des Scavans* [the two first scientific journals] was *not* the publishing of new scientific papers so much as the monitoring and digest of the learned publications and letters that were now too much for one man to cope with in his daily correspondence.

What I find fascinating, you see, is that we're really back to where we were three hundred years ago, for two reasons. First, a scientist can no longer keep up with all the journals, and second, researchers have now returned to letter writing and simply bypass the journals."

SNOW: "What got you interested in this?"

GAULEY: "Primarily, the National Science Foundation grant to the American Psychological Association for a national information system, and the controversy that resulted from it. Even though the preprint provision was struck from the proposal, the whole pattern of journal publication, as we have known it for three hundred years, has got to be affected and changed because of this grant. Quite frankly, I feel that psychology has led all the other sciences in the study of scientific communication. Just look at the massive APA studies in 1963 and 1965."

SNOW: "The gist of your article, then, would be to point out a need for a new form of publication to replace the journal as the basic vehicle for publishing the results of scientific research? A kind of 'Future of the Scientific Journal' type of piece."

GAULEY: "That's about it. The traditional journal just can't and doesn't meet today's needs. Even the American Institute of Physics recognizes that fact. Read Koch's 1970 AIP report where he describes the primary journals in physics as 'archival.' That's quite a major step from what Pasternach of AIP was saying just four years earlier. What he termed a 'danger'—that the primary journal was going to become an archive—is simply an accepted fact in Koch's report. You see, AIP realizes its journals are an archive, and an archive cannot be considered part of a *current* communication system in the sciences!"

SNOW: "Your argument centers on the long delays in the publication of journal articles?"

GAULEY: "Correct."

SNOW: "This is not a new phenomenon. The delays can be traced largely to the time needed for refereeing, editing, composition, corrections, typesetting, and printing. Even large infusions of money could not radically speed up the process. You call the end product, the journal, an 'archive,' but if a paper is to be included in an archive, it should be a contribution to the scientific world that's worth preserving. The very procedures you object to seem to me to be those that are essential to the publication of papers worth reading and worth preserving."

GAULEY: "That only leads us to the next problem with journals, and it is that they're just too thick for a scientist to have time to read. He may look through a whole issue of *Journal of Chemical Physics* and only read one article. Why should he have to subscribe to the whole journal, when he needs only a fraction? We've come to the point where it's impossible for a scientist to read, to pay for, or even hope to come into contact with all the significant literature in his specialty."

SNOW: "What do you see as the solution?"

GAULEY: "My solution is to recognize and accept the fact that we've reverted to the seventeenth century. The scientist cannot keep up with or use the journals effectively, so he's gone back to the letter, calling it a preprint. The biggest problem as I see it is that for three hundred years, the journal issue itself has been the primary means for dissemination. I find myself in great sympathy with the minority of scientists who, for over forty years, have been saying that the individual paper is what should be substituted. The old Scientific Information Institute, proposed in the thirties, is the prototype of what I have in mind. Authors would submit their papers to an institute, along with a summary. The summaries would be published quickly in journal form, and the full text of individual papers could be ordered from the institute, as needed, by individual scientists, probably at a much smaller annual cost than the current cost of a one year subscription to one of today's journals. This system would, of course, for all intents and purposes, mean the end of the journal as we know it."

SNOW: "There have been many proposals similar to the Watson-Davis plan you describe. On paper, they seem attractive, until it comes time to put the system into practice. But how could any one central depository hope to get cooperation from the whole scientific community? How could any one central agency distribute the required numbers of copies in even one country? And, what about the world demand for these papers? Could a central agency hope to satisfy it? You surely must see that, grand as this plan sounds on paper, in practice it would probably be less satisfactory than the present system."

GAULEY: "But we *have* had two successful preprint distribution systems, one in biochemistry and one in physics. Both systems supplemented the journals, yet met the need for really rapid distribution of experimental results. Both were killed by the journal editors in the respective fields, who claimed they were too much of a threat to the journals. Of course, that is all in the past, but the APA proposal contained a similar preprint distribution system, which was cut out before funding by NSF."

SNOW: "That was cut because the members of APA objected to it. The research psychologists called a massive preprint system of publication 'unprofessional,' and said it would lower the quality of published research."

GAULEY: "Could the technical report replace the journal? Would that format meet the methodological shortcomings that people object to with preprints? There are pretty good bibliographical controls and methods of distribution already set up and operating now for technical reports."

SNOW: "Reports are deceiving. The central technical reports distribution agency in this country handles only 50,000 new items a year and has a *total* retrospective collection of only 300,000 reports. We now generate over

600,000 journal articles each year, on a total base of about 7 million scientific papers since the beginning of 'science.' Technical reports raise many of the same problems as preprints do in that they are unedited, and so forth. Add to this that librarians have never been comfortable with technical reports, and I think it's a safe bet to conclude that we're far better off with journals."

GAULEY: "Then, perhaps, the ultimate solution to the whole problem would be to declare American scientific journals a national resource, and have federal control and distribution of scientific results like the Russians do. We're only a few steps away from that now."

SNOW: "What do you mean?"

GAULEY: "At the end of almost every scientific article, you find a statement that funds for the research came from some agency of the federal government. This research could be considered public property, and if so, why should citizens have to pay for a journal in order to make use of it?"

• • • • •

As a librarian, how would you assess the points of view of the two participants in this discussion? What support can be found in the literature for their individual views?

How do you view the future of the scientific journal? What is its current importance as a vehicle for dissemination of scientific information?

Which groups are engaged in planning national information systems at present? How are they funded? Would any of the projected national information systems fundamentally alter the current role of the scientific journal?

24

The Technical
Report Syndrome

· · · · · · · · · · ·

"Look at these photocopies! This one is from *Scientific and Technical Aerospace Reports* and this one is from *Nuclear Science Abstracts*—regional technical report centers scattered all over the country, all filled with technical reports!"

"Those are two swell-looking photocopies, L. C." said Don Mitchell, Assistant Engineering Librarian at Coyle University. "But why should I look at them?"

"Didn't you go to the staff association meeting? No, how could you? You're on reference in the afternoon. Let me fill you in. We're now making a big push to collect technical reports, the more the merrier. The director announced that because of the increase in government contracts at the university, the library has asked to be designated officially as a technical report center, and the engineering library will handle the reports," reported L. C. Boyer.

"Two questions. First, why get uptight? We only work here, and we simply carry out policies made by the administration. Second, technical reports are a legitimate vehicle for publication, and we already do our share of reference and acquisition of them. In short, why work yourself into a lather, when there's not one possible thing you could do to block what's going to happen."

"We can talk about it, can't we? I hate to think of this library crawling with technical reports. I agree with the guy who characterized them as 'bastard publications.' I think even the Weinberg Report mentioned that they're not worth keeping, unless they finally appear in a standard journal. Now, just as a for instance, assume *we* decided only to keep the ones that finally get published. Who'll correlate the published journal article with the report? Can you imagine trying to check every article in every journal that comes here to determine which ones were once technical reports? Then, somehow, we'd have to mark those reports as worthy of retention. Another problem is the sheer number of reports any center has to deal with. Clearinghouse, or National Technical Information Service, or whatever they'll call themselves tomorrow, are estimating that they handle about 30,000 new reports a year. Add to that AEC and NASA and you get a good fifty to sixty thousand reports annually."

"You did all this research in one night?"

"No, I did a paper on technical reports in library school and kept a copy. I feel like labelling it 'F.Y.I.' and sending it to the director."

"O.K. I've got time to listen, so give me your capsule summary on technical reports."

"Well, technical reports developed originally as a communications vehicle in World War II, because of the decentralization of scientific effort through research contracts. They were sent to the sponsoring agencies as progress reports or final reports, and then distributed to other scientists or officials with a great deal of security. After the war, captured German and Japanese research reports were circulated in a similar manner, again with a good deal of security, as opposed to open, general publication.

"With the tremendous growth of DOD after the war, and the creation of AEC and NASA, the technical report syndrome infected just about the whole scientific community to the point where it's become a publishing epidemic. There are supposed to be one million technical reports in existence. The report centers were established in the sixties as depositories for unclassified technical reports, with responsibility for reference, photocopying, and lending. Attacks on technical reports as a method of publication came mostly from journal publishers, who consider them a threat to their existence and . . ."

"Why are they a threat to journal publishers?"

"Eventually, many of them get published in journals. Now, if you had already read the report, would you read the journal article? Of course not, and you'd probably cancel your subscription to the journal as well. Besides the reports get published faster too and . . ."

"Too bad for the publishers of journals. If scientists prefer technical reports, they should be able to read technical reports. The old law of supply and demand!"

"Let me finish. The reports are not really finished products. In order to get published in a journal, they usually need extensive revision. Some reports get submitted for publication in reputable scientific journals, and others are just lost. Only the ones that do get published as journal articles ever enter the orderly chain of scientific communication."

"You sound like either a pompous ass or a future journal editor."

"Will you let me finish! I'm just giving you the view from both sides. Now, let's say a technical report is submitted to a journal for publication. Why should the journal publish something that is, in fact, *already published?* A report submitted for journal publication is a republication of data and can hardly be considered an original article. Also, reports are poorly indexed. Look at the last fifteen to twenty years of U.S. Government Research and Development Reports; no indexes for the vast majority of reports. Look at the reports themselves, unedited, unchecked, and unevaluated by scientific peers before publication. Technical reports constitute a vast wasteland of both good and bad material, most of which is irretrievable."

"Why are there so many reports if they're so bad?"

"Simple. Research contracts from the federal government state you must report on what you've done with the money you've been granted. So you write a report and submit it to the department or agency that's granted you the money. They publish the reports, distribute them to a limited number of interested people, send them to the report centers as sort of deposit copies, and offer them for sale to the general public through another agency."

"Your argument is that we shouldn't get involved collecting technical reports but should use the existing centers for our report needs? Your comments on the value and quality of technical reports as publications are personal opinions, based on research for a term paper. What *I* would really like to know is what do the people who use them think of them? After all, it's their opinion that really counts. So what if reports are poorly edited, or sketchily indexed? These people can read, and if they spot a bad report, they won't use the results. The problem of retrieval is ours, and we get paid reasonably well to find a report if we're asked."

"The only trouble with your argument, Don, is that we won't be asked. You're either on the mailing list of the government sponsor or not. Scientists don't browse through report collections or leaf through the report indexes. My objections to technical reports are objections to a method of publication. I'd much prefer to see authors of these reports take the journal route for publication. Then the contents are abstracted, indexed, edited, and judged by the people who use them. What's more, it's a fairer system for the science-technology people in that all get an equal shot at research results at the same time."

Coyle University's engineering library serves the students and faculty of the department of engineering as well as an associated center for advanced research in engineering (CARE). The recently established center has already attracted national recognition because of the quality of the applied research it conducts. Since CARE accepts only contracts that are not defense related, student acceptance of the center has been good. With 500 researchers and technicians on the staff, and with a significant number of students participating on the research projects, CARE is involved in eighty-two contracts ranging from transportation to nuclear reactor technology to low-cost urban housing.

The engineering library, with a staff of three professionals and a collection of 72,000 books and bound periodicals, was selected as the information center for CARE, as opposed to the creation of a new library at the center. A clerical assistant assigned to the center serves as a library resource person to expedite photocopying and loan of material for the staff. The grapevine at the library indicates that the pressure for improved access to report literature was generated by the staff of the center.

Don Mitchell and L. C. Boyer were classmates in library school. After graduation, both accepted positions at the library with the same title, assistant engineering librarian. It is not unusual for them to discuss professional issues at length in this way during off-duty hours.

• • • • •

Do you agree with L. C. Boyer's view on the technical report as a vehicle of publication? Does this library, by ordering or receiving technical reports, help perpetuate an inferior type of literature? What stake, if any, would librarians have in the reported conflict between the technical report and the journal article?

In your judgment, is this library a good candidate to become a regional technical report center? Where are these centers? Would it be better for the engineering library at Coyle to depend instead on existing centers to meet the information needs of the research staff at CARE?

25.
A Preprint
Is Not a Publication

. . . .

"Harv, have you seen the latest issue of *Biochemical and Biophysical Research Communications?* I checked the shelves where current issues are kept, but no luck."

"It's right here on the desk, Dr. Machey, in front of me. Someone just used it and I haven't had a chance to put it back yet."

"Oh, great! I just want to check the footnote style once more before I mail my paper in to them. Could I put these envelopes down on your desk a minute?"

"Here, let me help you. You sure do have a lot of correspondence."

"All but the large envelope are preprints of the paper I'm submitting to *BBRC.* I send the preprints out at the same time that I submit the paper. By exchanging preprints, my friends and I keep each other 'super-current'."

"Then, the paper to the journal will be on the editor's desk for quite a while?"

"Probably two months at the most, if they decide to publish it, but the preprint will be in circulation to forty-nine of my colleagues as fast as the mails can carry it."

"Perhaps you'd put the library on your list for preprint distribution? Of course, we'll get a copy when it comes out in the journal, so I suppose it's really not necessary for us to have it now."

"That's right, Harv. But meantime, I want the other boys to know what I'm doing. This prevents unnecessary duplication of research, and their overlapping into my experiments. On the other hand, someone might be as far along as I am, and we could get together and perhaps coauthor a paper."

"Doesn't distribution of the preprint constitute publication? Why bother with *BBRC?*"

"No. The preprint will only be cited as a personal communication by the authors who see and decide to use it. The *BBRC* paper is recognized as a publication, but only of the 'letters' type. However, it is a legitimate publication that can be cited by another scientist who sees fit to do so. In a way, the preprint and the letters journal accomplish the same thing, rapid communication."

"But the preprint is an illegitimate publication."

"Look, let me get these into the mail first, and then we'll discuss this some more if you'd like. I'll pick up a sandwich and a cup of coffee and bring it back, if you don't mind. Would you like coffee?"

"Please, cream and sugar."

The Institute for Biophysical and Biochemical Research is a nonprofit corporation devoted to research in nucleic acids and the genetic code. Operating on a budget which derives from a combination of federal funds and foundation grants, the Institute has been in operation for over twelve years, and has recently hired Harvey Slate as Librarian on a full-time basis. Mr. Slate reorganized the library during the past year while working there on a part-time basis, meantime holding the post of Science Librarian at a nearby college. Working nearly every Saturday, he arranged the book and journal collections of the Institute in a manner that requires little direct supervision by the librarian. Since many of the staff work very late in the evening, the pattern of a self-help library has seemed to best fit their needs. Mr. Slate began his new job two days ago. In it, he will be chiefly concerned with selection of new materials, and with borrowing necessary books and journals from other libraries as the immediate needs of the staff dictate.

"Here's your coffee, Harv," said Dr. Machey, returning with his coffee and sandwich in hand. "Now, let's see if I can give you the picture on the preprints/letters type publications. I suppose the most significant difference between the two is that the editors of the primary journals in the field accept letters publications as legitimate. Take that short communication I've just submitted to *BBRC*. At some point, say in six months, I'll write a full-length article on this topic. I'll be able to cite my *BBRC* paper in the full-length article, and, what's more, I'll probably receive some correspondence from the people who see the paper in the letters journals. This will help me polish the full-length article, which I will submit to a standard journal.

"My preprint is being sent to the people who I feel really will be interested in the research and from whom I'm most likely to get feedback. But the *BBRC* communication will be seen by many more people than the preprint. You see, then, that the preprint is not a publication. After all, publication can only occur in the professional journals in one's field. The danger with preprints is that they can be considered publications, and once that happens then no standard journal would ever publish them. Why should they, when they would only be republishing a preprint?"

"I see only a difference in terminology. The *BBRC* paper is published in abbreviated form, but it is nevertheless published. The preprint, as I see it, is really a privately published paper with yourself as publisher!"

"The preprint list I maintain has only forty-nine names on it, so you can see that it's not a publication. What it is is forty-nine copies of a personal letter, and no more. The *BBRC* publication will be edited to some extent and, most important, it will be retrievable in the literature. It will be indexed and abstracted in the appropriate sources, whereas the preprint I sent out can, for all intents and purposes, be considered lost to the scientific world."

"How does Information Exchange Group fit into the picture in relation to your preprint?"

"It doesn't. It's defunct."

"Then, perhaps I should ask what it *did* do?"

"It took the preprints in my field, and provided central duplication and dissemination to individuals who had signed up to receive a certain group of preprints."

"That sounds like a sensible way to handle the preprints. You said yourself the *BBRC* paper, even if accepted, will take about two months to get into print, but your forty-nine preprints will be in the hands of the recipients in a matter of three or four days."

"IEG *was* good in a way, but it was bad in many respects too. The fact is it lost funding and collapsed, but the standard journals are still here, doing their jobs as effectively as possible. I was a Group VII member of IEG as soon as it was formed, and must have received about a thousand preprints through this system. It became just too big to handle from an operational point of view, and it stirred up a hornets' nest in the communications process in the sciences. However, I think that it did force expansion and enlargement of the letters journals in all fields, not just biomedical."

"Then, there is an orderly process of communication in the sciences that just cannot be upset?"

"Right, Harv. What we're really back to is that you can't have your cake and eat it too."

• • • • •

How would you describe the "orderly process of communication in the sciences" that Mr. Slate refers to? Do you see the differences between letters journals and preprints in the same or different terms than Dr. Machey does? Would the IEG experiment ultimately have been beneficial to libraries of this type? Why did IEG fail? If IEG or a similar preprint distribution system began again, how would it affect this library? Why would the recipients of Dr. Machey's preprint properly cite it only as a personal communication, if they used it as a reference?

Are there other journals in the biomedical field besides *Biochemical and Biophysical Research Communications* to which Dr. Machey could have submitted this short research paper? Which are they?

26.
The Simplified Search

• • • • • • • • • • • • • • • •

"Is it in the little brown bag, Mr. Ruthland? Is that where it is?" asked Elizabeth Pinson, Assistant Engineering Librarian at Penola State College. "Mr. Ruthland, you simply must answer my questions, if I'm going to be able to help you search the patent literature. Why don't you shake your head 'yes' or 'no' to my questions, since you refuse to answer any direct questions about your invention? Do you have any idea of the class or subclass the invention would fall into? You don't? All right. Would you tell me the subject of the invention, the common name, process, or object that you've invented? If you can give me that information, then we'll be able to search the *Index of Classification* to find the class or subclass. Mr. Ruthland, you'll just have to trust me a little if you want help in searching the patent sources. Mr. Ruthland!"

"Take it easy, Beth, you're beginning to attract attention. Your voice has increased steadily in volume, since you began talking to that man," warned Phyllis Stanwood, Engineering Librarian.

"I'm really sorry," said Elizabeth, stepping away from Mr. Ruthland for a moment, "but he wants me to help him with the patent literature, and he won't even talk to me about what he wants to search. *None* of them will ever tell you what it is that they're thinking of patenting. Just look at the grip he has on that bag."

"Think of another way to handle the problem. I won't have the staff of this library engaging in verbal assaults on the patrons, whether they are college personnel or residents of the city. Under the rules of the library, each has a equal right to use the collection."

"The way patent literature is organized, a person would either have to be a librarian or a patent attorney to wade through it. They ought to simplify it, so that the Ruthlands of the world would have an easier time of it. Oh, now Mr. Ruthland's gone away again, and he's really such a nice person. I had lunch with him two weeks ago, and he's a delightful man, except when he's searching the patent literature. Did you know he actually has two or three patents in force now? One of them has something to do with sausages."

"Why don't you try to work out a system for the general public that would enable them to use the patent sources themselves?" asked Mrs. Stanwood.

"Sort of a programmed text, or a flow-chart type thing?" mused Beth. "Perhaps some kind of graphic explanation that would allow them to walk up to the patent area, and be put on a track, or series of tracks, leading them to the right section of the *Gazette* or the *Patent Index*. I really would like to try to do that."

"Fine. I expect we'll have more Mr. Ruthlands as the news of the open-door policy spreads."

Penola State College is a branch of a newly formed statewide system for higher education. Located in the largest city in the northern quadrant of the state, Penola Bay, which has a population of 62,000, this branch of the state system was formerly a private college with a strong undergraduate program in arts and sciences. Financial difficulties brought the private college to the brink of bankruptcy, at which point it was absorbed into the state system.

The engineering library at Penola State has two professionals on the staff and a collection numbering about 34,000 bound volumes. The collection also includes subscriptions to forty current engineering periodicals, as well as a substantial group of older technical reports. Most of the technical reports were collected when the college was the setting for a state agricultural experimental station. Newer reports are being added gradually in the engineering sciences both through purchase and by selection as deposit series, since the library at Penola has been designated a partial depository for U.S. government documents.

Penola Bay is an attractive, affluent community. When the state assumed administrative and financial control of the college, the libraries at Penola State were opened to the general public. Use of the library by area residents has been increasing steadily, week by week, ever since. Many actual and potential inventors are seemingly to be found among the citizens of Penola Bay, if one is to judge by the demands made on the collection of the engineering library, especially the use of the patent literature. This library has a complete collection of patent reference tools, and the nearby public library has an extensive set of patents, arranged in numerical order, from which copies of requested patents can be ordered. Just as Miss Pinson was considering how this literature might be made more accessible to the public, she was interrupted by the appearance of Professor Mitchell, a member of the college faculty, at the reference desk.

"Beth, did you see this article in the paper by a Washington consumer advisor? He claims that by increasing humidity, comfort can be obtained at lower temperatures."

"Does it have to do with the fuel shortages this winter?"

"Right. Of course, the article contains the standard advice on storm windows, fireplaces, and properly operating furnaces, which I don't find any cause to disagree with. But that statement that increased humidity in a home will require less heat is, I suspect, misinformed. A statement like that will sell more humidifiers, but I doubt it will reduce actual consumption of fuel. You see it says right here, 'with humidity at 45 to 50 percent, comfort can be obtained at temperatures of 68 to 75 degrees. When the humidity in the house drops to 25 percent, a heat level of 78 degrees is needed.' There are two problems with this. First, I doubt any humidifier could put out enough moisture to raise the humdity that high in any but the smallest of apartments, let alone houses. Second, I don't think the relationship between heat and humidity is at all as clearly established as is implied here."

"Would you like us to do a search on the heat-humidity statement?"

"That's it. Send up photocopies of a few relevant articles or paragraphs on the problem, if you can. I suppose they could be right, but I doubt it. Maybe you'd better locate a few more references."

●　●　●　●　●

Devise a self-help system for the patent literature that would satisfy the needs of the citizen-inventors who use the Penola engineering library. Consider the suggestion of a flow chart or programmed text. This system should allow for the possible variables of entry into a patent search, as well as for maximum privacy for the person searching.

Locate the information desired by Professor Mitchell through the most appropriate sources.

27.
The Verbosity Ratio

· · · · · · · · · · · ·

"Bourbaki, that's B–o–u–r–b–a–k–i."

"Faculty?"

"It says Professor N. Bourbaki."

"Fine," said Bob Willcox, Assistant Librarian at Nyland University Science Library, as he reached for the large, green *Nyland Staff Directory* on the desk.

"Oh, no, you've misunderstood me. Professor Bourbaki isn't a faculty member here. He wrote this article," said the student, holding up a bound volume of the *American Mathematical Monthly*. "I'd like to know something about him. You know, where he teaches now, what else he has written, that kind of material."

"No problem," smiled Willcox, as he reached for the latest copy of *American Men of Science,* and began leafing through the 'B' section. "No, he's not listed in here. Could I see the citation?"

"Sure. At the bottom of the page, it says he was a member of the Royal Poldavian Academy, so I suppose he's a foreigner," commented the student as he handed Volume 57 of the journal to Willcox.

"The title is 'The Architecture of Mathematics' by Nicholas Bourbaki, and this seems to indicate he's living in France. Would you mind starting to check some of the foreign biographical directories over there behind me? I'll be over to help you in just a few minutes," said Willcox, noting that two other students were waiting to ask questions.

"May I help you?" he asked the next student in line.

"Thanks. You've heard of the game, 'Instant Insanity'?"

"I recall the name, but that's it," said Willcox.

"One of the math journals is supposed to have published a solution for this game a while back. I'd like to read that, if I can find it."

"*Mathematical Reviews* is probably your best bet. You'll find it right over there, next to the current math journals. When you find the citation, come back, and I'll help you find the journal."

"Right over here, *Mathematical Reviews?*"

"Sure," said Willcox standing up and pointing to his left, "you can't miss it. It's that long red set of indexes, right there."

"I see it, thanks."

"I'm sorry you had to wait so long, but can I help you?" said Willcox to the next student.

"I think I'd better come back later, when you're no so busy, or make an appointment to see you some other time."

"That's not necessary. Sit down, and ask your question."

"All right. I'm a graduate student in the library school here, and I'd like to ask you a question about the literature of science and technology."

"I got out in '67, and my name's Bob Willcox."

"I'm Jane Simpson, and I hope to get out this year. Did you go to Nyland?"

"Right, and do you have McGregor for sci-tech?"

"Yes, and that's why I'm here. I've selected multiple authors of scientific papers as the topic for a paper I'm doing. Let me show you what I mean. Here's a copy of *Science,* a copy of *Physical Review, Section D* and a copy of *Physical Review Letters.* Now, they're all different years but let's take this '69 issue of *Science* as an example. First article, four authors; second article, six authors; and the third article, one author. In *Physical Review,*" said Jane, "I've marked this one here. Eleven authors! And in a two-page letter in *Physical Review Letters,* six authors!"

"On that last paper you pointed out, each author probably contributed two paragraphs. I believe that the phenomenon you're describing has been referred to in the literature as the 'verbosity ratio.' It's the ratio of words in an article to the number of authors."

"Why does this happen in scientific literature? What has happened to the present-day scientist that separates him from the likes of Galileo, Galton, Franklin, Boyle, and Brahe? Now they're grouped together like a herd! Could that be it? Are they afraid to stand alone on their work?"

"Let's cover one more outgrowth of what you asked about first, and that's another trend in the literature connected to this problem, but one you might overlook. Many-authored articles is one trend, but so is 'no-authored' articles."

"Articles without authors?"

"No personal authors. Instead, two or three laboratories would be listed as authors."

"I hadn't run across that at all. You say the two things are connected?"

"They are."

"I've done a very crude search of a couple of volumes of journals that are fifty years old, and it's clear that one and two-author articles were in the majority then. It seems now the trend has completely reversed itself, and one- or two-author papers are becoming increasingly rare. Something else I don't understand is this. On a multi-authored paper, how do you tell how much each person has contributed? Does the positioning of the names have anything to do with it? Why don't they rate each author's contribution to the article? Take that paper with eleven authors. How does one know who did what? Are they all equally responsible for the publication?"

"I'm sorry, but we're all going to leave the library for a while," said Willcox, standing and surveying the room.

"Leave?"

"That's right. That bell is the fire alarm. I have to get these students out of here before the safety engineering or the fire department arrive, and it's no easy job. The students don't like to leave for fire alarms unless the flames start licking their boots. Come on back after it's over, and we'll get at your questions."

The Science Library at Nyland University, one of the foremost universities in the nation, is a large and extremely well-managed scientific facility. Mr. Willcox, one of three assistant librarians, is presently the only professional on duty, because the others, including the librarian, have the flu, and are expected to be away from work at least a week.

• • • • •

Identify Nicholas Bourbaki and briefly list the publications he has to his credit.

If you were Bob Willcox, how would you answer the questions posed by Jane Simpson? Is there any connection between the publications of Nicholas Bourbaki and the phenomenon of multiple authorship of scientific papers?

Would you have responded to the 'Instant Insanity' question differently from Mr. Willcox?

28.
Pugwash et al.

• • • • • • • • • •

"Dr. Speight, Mrs. Land said I was to come to your office as soon as I got to work today," said Jim Mayer, newly appointed professional assistant at the Belem State University Library.

"Yes, come in and sit down, Jim," instructed Charles Speight, Director of Libraries at Belem. "I asked Mrs. Land to send you to my office to see if you would be willing to undertake a short project for me. You're probably aware of the conference we're having here in a couple of months on scientific communication. The man scheduled to deliver the keynote address has fallen and broken his leg. He asked to be replaced, but I felt that it's a little late for that, so I offered to help him in any way that I could. He is planning to speak on the need for a world scientific information center, and has asked me to provide him with some additional source material from the not too distant past. What I would like you to do is locate these references for him. If you're agreeable to this, I'll arrange with Mrs. Land that you'll be free to do the work."

"I'd like to try."

"Good. He says that he's already tried to find these items, without much success. The first is a conference paper by M. M. Dubinin entitled 'Needed: A World System of Scientific Information.' The conference was cited only as P-COSWA, but I made a phone call and now know that that stands for the Pugwash Conference on Science and World Affairs."

"Pugwash?"

"I'm curious about the name myself. Perhaps if you can locate the paper, you could find something on the history of the conference that will explain the name."

"Dubinin's paper appears in the proceedings of this conference?"

"Correct. The conference was held in Czechoslovakia.

"Next, he needs a Stowe Conference entitled 'International Cooperation in the Pure and Applied Sciences.' This was held in Stowe, Vermont in the 1960s."

"Should these conferences be purchased, or photocopies made of them, if we don't have them?"

"Do whatever you have to do to get either the originals or photocopies of both conferences, as quickly as possible, and bill the administration account for whatever charges are incurred."

"Both sound like routine searches for conference proceedings. I'll start on it right away."

"There's one more thing, and that's on the topic of conferences and conference proceedings in general. I wonder if you would, as a part of this project, produce a three or four page summary on conferences, their availability and value? We have no formal selection policy on conference material, and perhaps that is the best kind of policy to have. I'm wondering, and so is Mrs. Land, whether we should have a more formal policy on purchase of conference papers and proceedings."

"Would this be for just scientific conference proceedings?"

"Yes, I think it would be good to start in the scientific fields. Since we don't have a medical school here, you might eliminate medical conferences and congresses."

"Information on the number of conferences, the bibliographic control of conference papers, and the average cost of conference proceedings?"

"That's it. And perhaps the proportion of conference papers that are eventually published through more formal channels, such as journals. You see it may not be necessary to buy conference proceedings on a massive scale, if we eventually receive them in the journals. You might use the Dubinin paper as an example. See if it was ever published in journal form, or abstracted while it was in conference form."

"I wonder if I shouldn't consider using a more recent paper than Dubinin's to plot the publishing history of a conference paper?"

"Might not be a bad idea. I wouldn't use the American Chemical Society Conferences for this type of check, because of the formal series they have to take care of their conference papers."

"I can remember using the volumes from the *2nd International Conference on the Peaceful Uses of Atomic Energy*. I believe there were over 2,000 papers published in bound form within a year of the conference. This shows what can be done. I'm also interested in the ways in which conference publications are announced, or I should say, the way they're not announced. I'll get back to you on the two conference citations as soon as possible and follow that up with a brief report on the scientific conference publications."

NOTE: The library at Belem State University is to be considered as having a better than average science collection for purposes of this case, with particular strength in mathematics and physics.

• • • • •

Locate information about the Pugwash Conference on Science and World Affairs held in Czechoslovakia, and determine if the Dubinin paper is included in the proceedings. Is it likely that this library would have copies of the "Pugwash Conference?" If not, is there a quick alternative method of securing the Dubinin paper?

Identify the Stowe Conference on International Cooperation in the Pure and Applied Sciences. Estimate the cost of purchasing the proceedings of this conference.

Satisfy Dr. Speight's request for a short report on scientific conferences, their value, and availability. Identify the pertinent bibliographic tools that can be used to locate published conference proceedings. Are these sources different from those that announce scientific conferences and meetings?

29.
Priority of Discovery

. . . .

"Mr. Robbins?"

"I'll be with you in a minute, young lady," said the head of the reference department at Emerald State College, as he took off his winter jacket and hung it on the coat tree behind his desk. "Please sit down, and briefly tell me what you want. I don't mean to sound rude, but I'm here to do the last part of my inventory of the reference collection, and I've come in on my day off to do it."

"I was going to leave you a note, because I've noticed that you don't work on Saturdays. I'm an advanced placement student here," began Janice Coles, holding up her library identification card for Robbins to see, "and I'm in desperate need of help with my science club project on lightning rods. The topic I've been assigned is the discovery and development of the lightning rod. Now, Benjamin Franklin's name pops into everyone's mind as soon as you mention this invention, but that's not enough for us."

"Not enough?"

"No, we'd like to start with the kite experiment. I've checked several histories, and the same picture of Franklin, the hill, the boy, and the dog appears. But, you see, that's not a *photograph*, it's just an artist's conception. So, my first question is, did anyone see him do it? And the corollary to that question is, was he the *first* to do the kite experiment, and, if not, who was?"

"The question is whether we can prove that Franklin actually did the kite experiment? You want first-hand testimony that he did it, so you'd like to have a corroborating witness?"

"Sure, why not? I mean the whole thing could be just folklore! I suppose that everyone thinks he was the first to have the idea of sending a key up on a kite in a storm. I want to be able to prove or disprove the whole theory. I've an open mind on the question, really. I just want the facts about what happened."

"I won't be able to get to this today, but I'll see what I can find for you on Monday morning. It won't take long, because I'm sure that whole episode of the kite experiment in 1752 is well documented."

"I think, Mr. Robbins, that you may find that even in 1752 there was some speculation about whether he really was the first scientist to bring electricity from a cloud."

"Well, we'll see. Was there anything else?"

"Did he invent the lightning rod?"

"This sounds like it's going to be a waste of both my time and your time. I think that what you're asking could reliably be checked in an encyclopedia."

"Secondary source! I need primary source materials to the three questions."

"The Franklin Collection! Students are not allowed to handle many of the items in this collection, so I'm afraid this puts a different light on your questions, and also extends the amount of time I'll have to spend researching them. After all, I'm sure you're aware that I just couldn't spend all day in the rare book room. I'll have to spread the work out. And photocopying the appropriate pages of those volumes will take a good deal of time. We have to be careful so as not to damage any of the items in Professor Keego's collection. They're part of his estate, and we're not sure, well, not absolutely sure, that he's left these books to the library, though we do have the use of them."

"Just one more thing, Mr. Robbins. What did the scientists of Franklin's own day think of the invention of the lightning rod? Did they consider it a particularly distinguished invention or was it more like the 'pop top' opener on cans today?"

"I believe there was a patent on the lightning rod . . . ."

"Oh, that would be terrific evidence."

"Miss Coles, these questions do seem a little odd. I mean, you're challenging new areas as yet unchallenged by scholars. Franklin's political opinions have been discussed for many years, but his scientific achievements are generally accepted."

"Yes, but maybe some of his scientific achievements were reported a little too hastily. I want to try to get the facts with your help, of course."

"I'll leave whatever I can find for you on this desk under the blotter, in an envelope with your name on it, next Saturday."

"Thank you, Mr. Robbins."

The library at Emerald State College, though not particularly large, has been in existence for well over one hundred years, and has maintained continuous subscriptions to a significant number of periodicals in both the humanities and the sciences since it first opened. This library also contains a complete file of state newspapers on microfilm, some of which date back over one hundred years.

The Keego Collection on Benjamin Franklin was the personal working collection of a deceased faculty member at Emerald State, who had devoted many spare hours to his favorite political and scientific figure in colonial America. Although the collection does not contain any material not held in other libraries it does include numerous works about Franklin, many issues of scientific periodicals of the past and present, and a significant number of pamphlets. The collection is kept in the rare book room in order to protect it, until it officially becomes college property.

• • • • •

Can Mr. Robbins produce documentation to establish the identity of the first scientist to bring electricity from a cloud by means of the kite and key experiment? When Benjamin Franklin flew his celebrated kite in a Philadelphia field in 1752, were there any witnesses? Who invented the lightning rod, and was it considered a significant achievement by contemporaries? Can a patent be located on the lightning rod?

30.
A Reprint Subscription

• • • • • • • • • • • • • • • •

Davidson Junior College, a private coeducational school in its thirty-fifth year of continuous operation, has experienced a dramatic increase in enrollment since it first opened with twenty-three students. The current enrollment in the one-year and two-year programs totals in excess of seven hundred, with a majority of the students living on campus. The college currently offers one-year certificate programs for secretaries, keypunch operators, dental technicians, and library technicians, the newest of the programs. Two-year programs, leading to the associate degree, are offered in electronic data processing, medical laboratory technology, business administration, and basic studies. The basic studies program is intended primarily for students who plan to transfer to a four-year college. In recent years, an increasing number of Davidson students have transferred to neighboring Coyle University.

Instructional resources at Davidson are currently supplemented through a number of formal and informal cooperative arrangements with the university. For example, some of the teaching staff and laboratory facilities necessary for the dental technician program are made available through an affiliation between the junior college and the university's school of dentistry. In addition, several graduate students, especially from the departments of science and computing science, are employed as instructors in the Davidson programs. Use of the extensive libraries at Coyle is not provided for by any of the existing arrangements between the two schools, because of the acknowledged deficiencies in the library at Davidson and the consequent burden such an arrangement would impose on the university libraries.

The library at Davidson, a converted cafeteria, is grossly inadequate in terms of resources, staff, and seating capacity. All are aware of this, including the Librarian, Bruce Albert. Mr. Albert has been active in efforts to improve the library since he came to Davidson two years ago, and has managed some improvements in service to students and faculty. The cost of recent acquisition of twenty-five acres of land adjacent to the campus, considered by all to be of utmost importance to the future of the school, has curtailed his efforts to improve the library to a point where it could be considered at least marginally effective. Each department of the school, including the library, has been forced to reduce expenditures in order for the junior college to find funds to purchase the land for further expansion.

Student unhappiness with the library, often vocal in the past, was exacerbated during the past week when the library could not provide material needed for the general chemistry course. As an apparent result, several fires were set in metal wastepaper baskets in the library. *The Diary*, the student newspaper of Davidson College, reported the incident as follows:

BIAS CHARGED

Mr. Philip Ryland, Instructor in Chem I, charged today that the library discriminated against his request for material to be placed on the reserve shelves in the library. Noting that he requested thirty copies be made of an article which appeared in *Science* magazine a week before the students were assigned the reading, Ryland said that his request was rejected out of hand by the library. Ryland explained he feels this happened because he is a graduate student at Coyle and only a part-time instructor at the college. "For years," said Ryland, "the library has made multiple copies of articles for reserve, and now they're trying to tell me it can't be done any more." Ryland's course is extremely popular with the 130 students he has now, and was well received when he taught it last year. Mr. Ryland will receive his master's degree in chemistry at the end of this semester.

The Head of the Library, Bruce Albert, was not on campus when Ryland announced to the students in class that his request for the article had been rejected by the library. Albert was unavailable for comment.

Three separate fires, which caused no damage to the college library, were started by persons unknown shortly after Ryland's class was over. The head of the Coyle Fire Department said he and his men responded, because the heat of the fires triggered the alarm system on each occasion.

The Diary has learned that the insurance company that underwrites the college's policy has threatened to cancel, if the incidents continue.

In addition, WYYY, the student radio station at Coyle University, has told representatives of this paper that Mr. Albert has agreed to be interviewed on the station tonight at 8 p.m. about the Ryland incident.

A partial transcript of the interview between Bob Carpenter, student head of the news department at WYYY, and Bruce Albert is reproduced below:

CARPENTER: "Our guest this evening on 'Interview' is Bruce Albert, Head of the Library at Davidson Junior College. Mr. Albert has agreed to appear on this program, and explain the position of the library in the recent controversy that resulted in several fires being set in the Davidson Library. Mr. Albert, could you tell us exactly what Mr. Ryland asked the library to do for his class?"

ALBERT: "His request was for thirty photocopies of an article that appeared in the December 25, 1970 issue of a journal entitled *Science*. As I recall, the article was by Edward Arnet and was entitled 'Computer-Based Chemical Information Services'."

CARPENTER: "And the library refused to honor Mr. Ryland's request?"

ALBERT: "Yes, we did, or I should say my staff did, but they were acting under my instructions, and I was obeying the existing laws of the United States."

CARPENTER: "I'm not sure of what law you're referring to, Mr. Albert. Would you explain?"

ALBERT: "Certainly. I've brought the issue of the journal with me expressly for the purpose. *Science* is a copyrighted journal. You can see this right on the title page. 'Copyright, then the letter *c* in a circle, 1970 by the American Association for the Advancement of Science.' What this means to the library or to an individual is that legally a person is entitled to make only *one* photocopy of an article. This comes under the doctrine of 'fair use.' Any more than one copy is a violation of the law, and there are no exceptions to this rule."

CARPENTER: "So it is illegal to make any more than one copy. And did you explain this to Mr. Ryland?"

ALBERT: "A staff member explained this to Mr. Ryland, and explained our policy on multiple photocopies of articles. We asked Mr. Ryland to do one of two things. First, we asked him to give us a couple of weeks to order thirty reprints of the article from the publisher. We did this for two reasons: because it's much cheaper than photocopying, and because it is a legal method of securing multiple copies of a copyrighted article."

CARPENTER: "Did Mr. Ryland object to this method?"

ALBERT: "Yes, because of the delay, and this is when we offered him our second proposal. We offered to call the American Association for the Advancement of Science and the author, and ask permission to make thirty photocopies of the article in question. Again he refused, but this time because he just didn't believe us. I spoke to him and assured him that these were the only legal and proper ways to accomplish what he asked."

CARPENTER: "Could you explain what a reprint is for our listening audience?"

ALBERT: "Reprints, or offprints, as they are often called, are actually extra copies of an article made by the publisher from the printing plates, when the journal is printed. The cost is about a penny a page to purchase as opposed to seven and one-half cents for *us* to photocopy."

CARPENTER: "Isn't this copyright law violated every day by almost every library?"

ALBERT: "Your question sounds like, 'don't most people cheat on their income tax?' The fact is that where copyright is violated, the law is violated. Quite frankly, our library is not particularly well supported at present. Someday we will be, and then we will hope to be able to afford all the journal subscriptions we require. Excessive photocopying, especially the grossly illegal kind such as Mr. Ryland suggested, just drives the cost of periodicals higher and higher. This puts libraries like mine, which are trying to catch up, further and further behind by constantly increasing the price of journals. So, as an example, we stopped this illegal practice of multiple copies of copyrighted material. Let me add here, we will still make a single copy of an article and put it on reserve for faculty anytime. All departments at the college were informed of this decision in the late summer, and many placed orders for reprints or extra copies."

CARPENTER: "I've never noticed, and I'm sure many of our listening audience have never seen, reprints in the Coyle Libraries. Do you make extensive use of reprints at your library?"

ALBERT: "First, let me say that the Coyle Libraries are very well supported and administered, so that most of the people using your libraries wouldn't be too familiar with the reprint. However, I am sure that many of your faculty and graduate students send for them when they want a copy of an article for their personal files."

CARPENTER: "Instead of making a photocopy?"

ALBERT: "That's right. Reprints are professionally produced, so naturally they look just like the periodical article. Reprints are also free, when requested from the author, so you see the other advantage. I am sure that countless thousands of researchers have reprint cards, and request copies of articles in this way."

CARPENTER: "May I ask who supplies these reprints to the authors?"

ALBERT: "Each journal has its own policy. For instance, some journals will send the author of an article 50 to 100 reprints free. Any extras have to be ordered and paid for. Other journals, like *Science*, don't send free reprints to the authors, but include an order form, so that 50 to 500 reprints may be ordered at very reasonable prices. In addition, some reprints are kept at the editorial office of a journal to fill such orders as we would have been happy to make for Mr. Ryland."

CARPENTER: "Seems like it would be simpler to photocopy them and have the copies immediately."

ALBERT: "It's quicker to photocopy an article, and legal to make a single copy for your use, but more expensive. With our budget, we have had to improvise. For instance, in the sciences we keep what I call 'reprint subscriptions' to several very expensive scientific journals. We subscribe to an index called *Current Contents*, and order a reprint of every article in several journals. In this way, we have coverage in areas we just couldn't afford to purchase in!"

CARPENTER: "Is this legal?"

ALBERT: "Oh, yes."

CARPENTER: "Could we turn our attention to the fires that were started as a result of this whole episode . . ."

* * * * *

Are Albert's statements on the illegality of multiple photocopies of copyrighted periodicals accurate for an educational institution? Is Albert's contention that there are no exceptions to this rule true? Has illegal photocopying had an effect on the subscription rate of scientific periodicals? Would you support Albert's refusal of Ryland's request for the Arnet article?

Is Albert's system of a "reprint subscription" a widespread phenomenon? Do you feel that this is a satisfactory method of securing subscriptions to periodicals that are not within the budgetary limitations of the Davidson Junior College Library?

31.
In Translation

· · · · · · · · · ·

The latest census data show that the city of Rexdale has a population of 55,000, an increase of 9 percent over the figure for ten years ago. Census figures also indicate a median income of $9,100 and a median number of school years completed of 12.3 for those over twenty-five years of age. The number of residents reported to be of foreign stock is recorded at one-third of the total population, and the number of foreign-born has increased to one-eighth of the population.

The residents of this suburban community are becoming increasingly aware of a new problem facing the city, because of an influx of the foreign-born, particularly those from Greece and Italy. In the past five years, the number of foreign-born residents of this city, located ten miles from one of the cultural and educational centers in the United States, has increased dramatically. The crux of the problem seems to lie in the lack of language facility.

The public schools face the problem of a growing number of children entering the system with a language barrier between them and their teachers. At present, the problem is centered at the elementary level, where the offspring of the foreign-born residents have become a sizeable fraction of the total enrollment at three neighborhood elementary schools. School officials have been hard pressed to find bilingual teachers and materials to meet the special needs of these pupils.

The language problem is particularly acute in the sciences, because of the difficult terminology, especially at the fourth grade level. In the following memorandum, Agnes Hayes, Elementary Science Coordinator, asks one of the elementary school librarians to help with part of the problem:

Dear Helen:

    I need help in trying to solve one specific problem faced by the teachers in our elementary schools, because of the lack of English facility of most of the Greek and Italian children. I have completed my survey of the fourth grade teachers, and have decided to begin at this level in the science area, which is proving to be the most difficult for them to handle.

The fourth grade science text in the series we use, the Silver Burdet Series, by Mallinson, deals with earth science. The teachers and I have decided that a translation of this volume would be of inestimable help to the children with obvious language difficulties. My hope is that you will be able to locate translations of this book for us in both Italian and Greek. In your search, please keep in mind our growing need for a Spanish translation of this same book.

Of course, we would not be able to afford a translation for each child. We hope that the library in each elementary school could be stocked with the translations, when and if you can locate them. This way, when a chapter or group of pages is assigned, the children could go to the library and use both the English and translated versions of the text.

Regards,

Agnes Hayes

In each elementary school, a room has been designated as the library. Helen Guthrie, in charge of three of these libraries, spends a portion of her time in each school daily. This arrangement is the best the school department could manage under existing budget limitations. The three neighborhood schools she serves have the largest proportion of children with language problems.

• • • • •

Explain in detail how you would locate the needed translations of this fourth grade science text. If translations cannot be found, what alternatives exist for solving the problem?

Should consideration be given to having this volume translated into both languages, and possibly Spanish, and then privately reproduced in order to secure needed library copies?

32

A Tightening Budget

· · · · · · · · · · · · · ·

The proposal to include a library in the new Ashford College science building was fought and fought hard more than five years ago. When the science building was in the planning stage, Dr. E. A. Hadlock, Director of Libraries, strongly stated his preference for retaining a single central collection rather than beginning the process of fragmentation of library services. His budgetary projections made it clear to the college planning committee that the decision to include a library in the building would result in added and increasing expense as the years passed. The science faculty, with equal zeal, insisted on a separate science library despite the proximity of the central library to the proposed science building. When it was finally decided to have a library in the new building, Dr. Hadlock agreed to support of the projected departmental library, and set out to hire a science librarian for it a year before the building was to be completed.

Charles Wendell was the unanimous choice of the director and the library committee for the new post. Mr. Wendell came to Ashford with several years administrative experience as Associate Science Librarian at a large university. His tenure as science librarian began twelve months before the completion of the building, when he immediately set about planning the physical location of materials in the new library and expanding the science collections. More than 5,000 new and standard titles were purchased just before the building opened, with the wholehearted approval of the faculty library committee for the sciences.

In the first three years, the growth of the science collections was dramatic, reflecting in part the substandard book and periodical resources previously available to the science faculty. The volume count increased from 16,000 to 32,000 and the number of subscriptions from 330 to 660, because of the substantial supplementary budget Dr. Hadlock had secured for the new library. This year, the fourth since the opening of the science library, the $36,000 book and journal budget represents something of a leveling off in acquisitions, but Wendell has been authorized to add a full-time reference librarian to his staff.

In his proposed budget for the coming fiscal year, Wendell has asked for funds to construct twelve closed faculty carrels in the library, as well as making the usual requests for increased book, journal, and bindery funds, even though he is aware of the gloomy financial outlook at the college. Conversations with the faculty library committee as well as other members of the faculty have led him to anticipate a year of little or no progress as far as increased funding is concerned. He, like other administrators on the Ashford campus, is aware of a recent decision that any necessary budget cuts will be applied to all units on an equal basis.

These thoughts passed through his mind, as he walked the short distance to the main library for his annual budget meeting with Dr. Hadlock. After he and the director had exchanged the usual pleasantries, Hadlock began discussing budget figures for the coming year: "Charles, let me begin with the obvious. The College Budget Committee, at the direction of the President's Office, has trimmed everyone's budget request across the board, right back to last year's level."

"No increases at all?"

"Very selective, very small increases in library materials budgets," said Hadlock. "Let me show you what I've been given for your library. Of course, the construction of the carrels and the new clerical position you wanted have been cut. No increases in binding or journals. A $250 increase in your book budget based on the strong recommendations you made, and seconded by the faculty library committee. That's a total materials budget of $36,250, with a clear understanding that *no* overexpenditures will be tolerated in any category."

"Unbelievable!"

"Here are the figures for the main library. You can see that they're proportional to what you received. My discretionary fund has also been eliminated, so that my hands are tied, and I will have no way to help you, or myself, for that matter."

"It can't be done! A frozen budget does *not* mean 'the same as last year.' It means *less!*"

"I know, but you know we are not alone. It's campus-wide. I've seen all the figures myself. Salaries look a little better, as a result of the cuts, but not that much better."

"Naturally, I'll appreciate a raise, but my concern is for the libraries. I'm afraid we'll have to cancel subscriptions."

"I've explained to the President that the level of service will be affected by these cuts. He acknowledged that fact, and reminded me that the last three or four years have been good ones for the college as well as the libraries, but the time has come to tighten our belts. He says the money is just not there."

"Do you mind if I think about what you've said, and try to come back with a few suggestions? I'd like to discuss what you've told me with Hilary, and see if we can come up with any workable solution."

"Fine, but remember, we've had years like this one before, and we've always sprung back. Don't let it get to you."

Wendell walked back to the science library slowly, pleased with his raise, but bitter about the cuts in the materials budget. His assistant, Hilary Coden, had been working for several months on the list of periodical titles currently received, and after much consultation with the faculty, had added and dropped nearly 100 titles. The total figure of 660 titles was not impressive in itself, but it did meet most of the major instructional needs of the department of science.

Hilary was naturally disappointed by the news about the budget, but not without ideas for meeting the crisis head on. "Let's just figure out what to do," she said. "First, it's quite obvious that we won't be able to continue all our subscriptions. We'll have to cut the appropriate number of titles to meet the rise in cost of the ones we keep. We've enough time to cancel, and we've only the single-year subscriptions with which to deal, so we have maximum flexibility at a time when we need it."

"That wasn't a bad idea, the single-year subscriptions. If we had expanded the journal collection in the second year of operation the way we did, *and* opted for three-year renewals instead of the single-year, we'd be in for a really large bill this year."

"Why did you decide against three-year subscriptions, anyway?"

"Past experience, I guess. If you go in heavily for the three-year renewals, the fourth year, when they're due again, you find yourself with a tough budget item and a difficult budget projection to plan."

"How does 15 percent sound to you as an estimated increase in scientific periodical subscription rates for next year?"

"Reasonable."

"Then, we need to cancel whatever number of titles adds up to 15 percent of the budget, and we've made it."

"But which titles?"

"From my studies of the publication lists of the members of this department, I'd say the reviews."

"The 'Progress in . . .' 'Advances in . . .' series?"

"No, the review journals, like *Reviews of Modern Physics.*"

"Why that type of journal?"

"Two reasons: first, the faculty here never publish in them, and second, those journals are all getting smaller. Add to that the fact that even though they're getting smaller, their prices are going up at an astonishing rate."

"I don't think that would be very wise. The review journal is a valuable tool that boils down research into critically evaluated summaries. That kind of publication deserves our support. Why don't we apply Bradford's Law to our collection, and check to see how many of our titles are on the periphery of more important journals?"

"Bradford's Law?"

"Samuel Bradford demonstrated that a relatively few journals carry a high percentage of the really important scientific articles. Just for purposes of demonstration, let's call that group Area I. Next, comes a group of journals, clearly secondary to Area I publications, but still carrying a significant number of important articles. We'll call these Area II journals. The next group of journals is clearly less important and carries few, if any, important articles. We'll call them Area III journals. You see what I mean about applying Bradford's Law to decide which journals should be cancelled?"

"I do, Charles, but what would you say if I told you I think we have a lot of Area II and III authors at this college? You're suggesting that we cancel journals our faculty publish in, and that would be a foolish thing to do."

"Cancelling the review journals is cutting the support for crucial publications. I just can't see it! Though it would simplify explanations to the faculty. We could just say that we had to cancel *all* the review journals, because of budgetary limitations."

"Look, they're getting smaller as the disciplines get larger, so they can't be that crucial. If they're getting smaller, and I mean number of pages, then that means fewer articles by fewer authors. I'll bet lots of other libraries will be thinking about dropping them, now that money is tight. By cancelling now, we're probably just ahead of the deluge of those who see the same pattern."

• • • • •

Is Wendell's proposed application of Bradford's Law to this particular problem in the Ashford College Science Library valid? Wendell states that review journals critically summarize advances in sciences, while Coden observes that as the literature increases, the size of the review journal tends to decrease. Are both these observations correct? If so, how can this apparent contradiction be reconciled?

Faced with the fact of a frozen journal budget and increased subscription rates, which proposal, Wendell's or Coden's, would you favor? If, in your judgment, neither seems a sound decision, what would be a better alternative?

APPENDIX

A partial list of review journals presently received in the Ashford Science Library:

Review of Scientific Instruments
Reviews of Modern Physics
Reviews of Plasma Physics
Reviews of Pure and Applied Chemistry

33.
The Results of a Survey

. . . .

"I sent my report up to you last week. I hope you found time to look at it," said Stan Martin, Assistant to the Director of Libraries on special assignment to the science library.

"Stan, I saw it come in, and made a note to myself to read it, but just never got around to it. As a matter of fact, I've completely drawn a blank as to why we made the survey," announced Robert Luray, Assistant Professor of Chemistry and chairman of that department's library committee.

"You recall the request sent by your committee to the science library for purchase of some forty-odd volumes of Gmelin's *Handbuch der Anorganischen Chemie*? I hope I pronounced that correctly."

"Oh, sure, I remember. About $5,000, wasn't it?"

"That's it. Well, in response to that request, we've asked each member of the faculty, and each graduate student, to answer two questions, just to get an idea of cost versus use. The first question asked was, 'Are you familiar enough with the organization of Beilstein and/or Gmelin to be able to use the source(s)?' Question two asked each of those surveyed to estimate his average use of each source in a year's time."

"I'm sorry to appear ignorant of your efforts, but I've really been tied up. I recall the whole thing now, and I have the time, if you have, to discuss it. Why don't you just tell me what you feel are the significant parts of this report?"

"If you'll turn to page nine of the report, you'll find Tables III and IV, the student-faculty responses to the two questions." [These tables are reproduced as an Appendix to this case study.]

"I have them. Let's see, eleven of the eighteen faculty responded to the survey. That's about 60 percent response."

"If we could backtrack a little, I have some figures here showing that the science library, to date, has spent about $15,000 on these two sets of chemistry reference sources. That, of course, does not include the proposed $5,000 purchase."

"I see our four organic chemists use *Beilstein* quite frequently, but only two people use *Gmelin* more than once a year."

"With a maximum use of six to nine times."

"So, you feel it would be unwise to buy more volumes of the *Gmelin* under these circumstances?" asked Professor Luray.

"No, not necessarily. I wouldn't draw that conclusion just yet. Let's go to Table IV, the responses by twenty of the thirty-three students, which I think, comes close to another 60 percent response."

"Here, Stan, you'll have to keep in mind that a third of our grad students are in their first year, and haven't started their research yet, so they'll have little use for either source. It seems clear that a majority don't know how to use either source. Those students that do probably work with a faculty member who uses it. In other words, I would see a connection between faculty use and graduate student use. A theoretical chemist, for instance, wouldn't use either source, so the students working under him wouldn't either. You see what I mean?"

"Yes, but 85 percent of the students responding didn't know how to use *Gmelin,* and 55 percent of the respondees did not know how to use *Beilstein!*"

"Look, Stan, I'll pass this on to the committee, and you ask your boss to hold up on the purchase of those additional volumes of *Gmelin* for a while. I'm not sure that it makes a great deal of difference how many times a source is used, as to whether the library should or should not have a new edition. Unless, of course, this were done for all other items in the library as well, but it's something the committee might want to take into account. If we don't buy the new *Gmelin,* we would certainly have a rift in the department, you know, the organics versus the inorganics."

"I had no idea it would become a political football!"

"It's going to be, either way."

"I was lost when I started this project, because of the subject matter, and now you've lost me again."

"The purchase of *Gmelin* is one problem. My bet is that the committee will vote to buy it, because any good science library should have these sources. Your survey points up another problem, one that's been a pet peeve of mine since I came to this university. Our department simply chooses to ignore the literature needs of the students, and your survey has added a little fuel to that particular fire. How can a student get a master's or a doctoral degree and not even have a nodding acquaintance with these two sources? How is it? That's what I've asked for the past three years, but nobody else in the department seems to care."

"While doing this study, I decided that you chemists are so specialized that you need only have knowledge of your specialty. I mean, you have your chem journals, colleagues, and information sources, but all within quite narrow boundaries."

"What you say is true, but would we buy a piece of equipment, and then not teach a student how to use it? Of course not, because implied in the purchase is the assurance the student will be taught the proper use of the equipment. The literature of chemistry, all of it, is another basic tool. When I went to school, a generation ago, we were taught the chemical literature for a semester in a one or two credit course. My experience both in industry and here leads me to believe that this literature course was one of the most important courses I ever took."

"Would you see the teachers of this course as being members of the chemistry department?"

"That's one possibility. On the other hand, I've been to quite a few faculty meetings, and I've heard the director of libraries argue, quite effectively, that librarians should be given full academic status. Not just the same health plan, or faculty club privileges, or rank, but the freedom, research, publication, and teaching responsibilities as well."

"Are you thinking of a librarian teaching the course to the Chem grad students?"

"Why not? The science librarian and his assistants handle the literature on a daily basis. As I talk to you, and my thoughts begin to jell, it seems like a better idea."

"There is the question of qualifications to teach such a course. The present science librarian does have a degree in plant physiology, but if I recall correctly, his B.S. was awarded in 1939."

"A chemical literature course wouldn't have to be mostly chemistry. It could very well be heavily used literature. Journals, indexes, etc. What about page charges, style manuals, technical reports, and the like?"

"Could I make another suggestion?"

"Go ahead."

"Why not issue each graduate chemistry student a handbook? When I started the survey, *Gmelin* and *Beilstein* were just two foreign-sounding names. Now, I know what they are, and how they're used. Just fiddling around one day, I used one book by Bottle, one by Mellon, and one put out by the American Chemical Society. All were really good. As a matter of fact, I took the ACS one home and read it. After I'd finished it, I felt I had really learned something about a field I'd thought most formidable. I suppose you could say that just giving the students a handbook would do the job, but if it were coupled with a one or two hour examination, the material would certainly be learned. As a matter of fact, all three of the handbooks do a really fine job on *Gmelin* and *Beilstein.* "

"Are you allowed to do special projects for faculty?"

"I was told to follow this project through to the end."

"Why don't you find out what ever happened to the formal literature course in chemistry, not just here, but at other colleges and universities? I wonder, too, if we could check to see if ACS has an official policy on the subject? Hell, if the faculty or the librarians don't *teach* the students how to use the literature, how's a student supposed to learn it?"

The Science Library at Russel University is not large, having only two professional librarians on the staff. Some years ago, an informal, mimeographed sheet with thirty-five questions relating to the chemical literature was handed to each new graduate student in the chemistry department midway through the first semester by the department secretary. The students were instructed to go to the library, and locate answers to the questions. Once in the library, they usually approached one of the librarians, and asked help in locating the answers. The questions, in the final analysis, served to give the librarians a finer grounding in the literature, but were considered merely of nuisance value by the graduate students. But ten years ago, even this modest attempt to acquaint the students with the literature was abandoned.

Stan Martin is one of two assistants to the director of libraries whose prime task is to undertake projects as special needs arise. The proposed purchase of supplementary volumes to *Gmelin* occasioned a supplementary budget request by the science librarian, and the subsequent cost/use evaluation of the source. The position held by Martin is considered an entering position in the Russel University Library system where a new employee can expect a variety of assignments.

• • • • •

After considering the results of Martin's cost/use study, do you feel this library should purchase the requested supplements to *Gmelin?* Do you agree with Professor Luray's statement that any good science library must have *Gmelin* and *Beilstein* in the collection?

What factors led to the demise of the literature course as part of the graduate curricula of most chemistry departments? Do you feel the trend away from teaching the literature of chemistry as part of the course work for graduate students is inevitable? Is it desirable? What is ACS's official policy on a literature course for chemistry graduate students? Evaluate Martin's suggestion that each graduate student in the Russel University Chemistry Department be given a copy of one of the handbooks, and an examination, in lieu of a formal course. Professor Luray suggests that the librarians, who seek true academic status, could be the ones to teach a formal course in the chemical literature. Would you agree?

APPENDIX

TABLE III
Faculty Responses (11 of 18 Faculty Members Responding)

Question 1 (Familiarity with *Beilstein* and/or *Gmelin*)

Beilstein:	10 Yes	1 No	
Gmelin:	9 Yes	2 No	

Question 2 (Frequency of use)

Average Use per Year	*Beilstein*	*Gmelin*
0–1	5	7
2–5	1	1
6–9	–	1
10	2	–
15	1	–
20	1	–

TABLE IV
Graduate Student Responses (20 of 33 Students Responding)

Question 1 (Familiarity with *Beilstein* and/or *Gmelin*)

Beilstein:	9 Yes	11 No	
Gmelin:	3 Yes	17 No	

Question 2 (Frequency of use)

Average Use per Year	*Beilstein*	*Gmelin*
0–1	2	–
2–5	3	1
6–9	–	–
10	–	1
15	–	–
20	2	–

"Mrs. Thetford, I'm Andrew Hull."

"Oh yes, Professor Hull, I read about your appointment to our faculty several weeks ago. It's a pleasure to meet you and have you here at Torun, after all the years of correspondence we've had."

"I'll tell you quite frankly, Mrs. Thetford, one of the most important factors in my coming to this university was the fine scientific collection and the excellence of your library service. Just your putting me on the mailing list for your *New Books List* made a great difference in the quality of the library I've been using, where I taught before coming here."

"How's that, Professor Hull?"

"When I received your monthly list of new books, I'd go to our library, check the catalog, and order anything on your list we didn't have."

"Just in your own subject area?"

"Oh, no! Well, maybe at first I just covered the physics books, but later I started covering the whole list. Physics, like other subjects, is becoming more interdisciplinary, and physicists have a great need to see books and journals outside of the field."

"That kind of procedure certainly places quite a responsibility on us."

"Well, after all, this *is* one of the centers of physics in this country. I might add that over the years, our library finally responded to the challenge. As time passed, I found myself having to write out fewer and fewer order cards. I suppose I pressured them into being more responsible about selection, but I feel they're better for it."

"Now that you're a member of the Torun University faculty, I hope you'll make even greater use of our library. Quite frankly, Professor Hull, I've used many of your letters of inquiry to this library as practice for my beginning reference specialists. Some of those letters required a good deal of searching, and in the process they exposed my staff to a great many sources in the scientific literature. So you see, we helped one another out without even knowing it."

"Very good. I've another pet project that I've been working on by myself for some time, and I'd appreciate some help now. You would, I'm sure, be familiar with the physicist, A. d'Abro?"

"Yes, we have several of his books in the library."

"Of course you do, and so do most libraries. Let me tell you all I know about him, and see what you can develop for me in the way of additional information. In 1927, he wrote *The Evolution of Scientific Thought from Newton to Einstein.* This book came out as a Dover reprint in 1950. In '39, he published *The Decline of Mechanism in Modern Physics.* This book became *The Rise of the New Physics; Its Mathematics and Physical Theories,* when Dover also republished it, in a second revised edition, in 1952."

"That seems like quite a bit of information to me."

"On the surface it does, but the problem is that we know him only through what he has written. I can find *nothing* out about the man—where he received his degrees, what professional organizations he belongs to, where he lives, or what he's writing now."

"Biographical information, then?"

"All the information on him you can muster. I can't even find out what journals he's published in!"

"We should have the reference sources and staff to handle that for you. I'll phone you as soon as we've located the information."

"One more thing. I'd like to register my current research project with whomever registers such projects. I think it's a Washington based service, probably a part of the federal government, that handles this type of registration. I'm not asking you to register for me, but only to find out whom I register with."

"Register for what?"

"I've some planned research, and some current work that I would like people in my field to be aware of. This Washington group tells whoever asks who's got what planned, and who's working on what current projects. The idea, of course, is to prevent unnecessary duplication. I got all this information on the phone from a colleague a few days ago, but he didn't have any details."

"I think that's called the National Register of Scientists and Scientific Projects Current and Planned, but we'll have to dig out the details on registration procedures and so forth for you."

"If I had asked the people at the library where I've been teaching these questions, they would have made me feel guilty, as they often did, for asking. You got the impression that you were interfering with their work day, when you asked for help with a problem. Here, you seem to thrive on such questions."

"Thank you, Professor Hull, but the accolades should be directed to our three professional assistants, and to the rest of the staff, who keep this library going. This is a team effort."

"Much like my branch of physics is."

The Torun University Science Library deserves all the praise it received from Professor Hull, for it is, indeed, a well-managed and fully equipped facility. This library has a particularly complete biographical collection, including many foreign biographical sources. Among these are *American Men of Science*, *Dictionary of Scientific Biography*, *Directory of British Scientists*, and Poggendorff's *Biographischliterarisches Handworten-buch zur Geschichte der exacten Wissenschaften*. A check of the card catalog reveals that copies of all four volumes by d'Abro are included in the collection.

· · · · ·

What comments would you have on Professor Hull's reported use of the Torun Science Library's *New Books List* as a selection aid? Locate biographical information on d'Abro for Professor Hull. Who sponsors the national register of scientific projects referred to? What specific service does it offer? Will Professor Hull be required to pay a registration fee to use it? Does the registry list both scientists and scientific projects?

35.
Science Fair

. . . .

Burford, a residential community with a population of 32,581, is not an affluent town. The personnel in each department of the town government must work diligently to ensure that, for each tax dollar expended, an equal amount of goods or services is returned to the town. The salary demands of town employees, which have been vigorously prosecuted under the collective bargaining laws of the state, have severely strained the financial resources of this largely middle class community. A four million dollar high school, now three years old, represents probably the last major financial expenditure this town can be expected to make for many years to come.

Slightly more than 1,000 students attend Burford High School in grades nine through twelve. This represents almost the entire population of Burford in this age group, except for a few students who attend a regional vocational high school. The school library, the first in any of the Burford schools, is open only on regular school days, between 8 a.m. and 3:30 p.m. On weekends and during school vacation periods, the library is not available for student use, although Jean Warden, the school librarian, is under contract to work a full month after school officially closes for the summer recess. The 8,950 volumes currently on the shelves have all been purchased since the 110-seat library opened three years ago. The library maintains subscriptions to sixty-two periodicals.

Three months ago, the department of science at Burford High held a science fair, the first in ten years. The winner of this fair represented the school at the regional science fair. The Burford entry won tenth prize in the regional event, and this performance rekindled an interest in the local science fair. Coincidentally, the winner of the local fair was awarded a full four-year scholarship to a neighboring university one month after receiving tenth honors in the regional fair. Soon afterwards, several parents appeared at a school board meeting, asking that funds be made available for an expanded science fair. These parents appeared particularly concerned by their children's reports of a notable lack of materials in the school library, either to locate or to support an appropriate topic. The parents, discounting the local public library because of its meager collection, wrote several letters to the town's weekly newspaper in an attempt to encourage greater support of the next science fair.

Subsequently, at Burford High, Charles Patch, Chairman of the Department of Science, and Jean Warden met to discuss the fair planned for the coming year.

"I don't know, Jean. If we had *planned* the fair, it probably wouldn't have worked out as well."

"It wasn't planned?"

"No, the science club asked for a fair at one of their meetings. I agreed, but I warned them that no one in the school was prepared for a science fair. They asked for a limited fair, a one year try, and said they'd carry the ball. We got twelve entries, and, as you know, our winner did quite well in the regional fair."

"I was a little surprised by the sudden requests for project material, and a little mad that we hadn't met to discuss it before it happened. I mean, we always have planned for events like this, or course changes, together."

"Well, that's past. So let's plan ahead now. Damn it, I'm due at a National Science Foundation institute for science teachers in two weeks, and . . . well, could you carry the ball for me? I'd ask some other science faculty to help, but they're headed for a well-deserved rest. You know darn well that the students and the teachers have just about had it at this point in the year."

"I'm not trained in the sciences, and never entered a science fair. I will do the best I can with what I have, but, Charles, I don't have any money for a special collection, or special emphasis on science fair projects. I can't get the library ready for next year's fair unless you can get the money to make it possible."

"Great, and not so great. The parents of the science club members have been making their interest in the next fair known both to me and, from what I hear, to the superintendent. We can't lose anything by sending a request for a supplemental budget to the principal's office. I know he'll send it on to the 'super,' and I figure we've got the money."

"Slow down. What are we trying for in this fair, numbers, or a few excellent projects? I guess I want to know your 'philosophy' on fairs for this school."

"It's been ten years since the previous fairs, and I was really surprised to find that this school had so little interest in them, when I arrived five years ago. Nobody, but nobody, was interested at that time! This sounds evasive, but I'll settle for a little of both. This is a hell of a way to run a ship, but I'm due in Florida in two weeks with wife, kids, car, and dog. You do whatever you think best, and we'll live with it for one year. I'll have a supplementary budget request typed up for us both to sign, and we'll send it off."

"O.K., Charles. Remember, we'll live with it."

A week later, Jean Warden found a note in her mail slot in the teachers' room which read as follows:

BURFORD HIGH SCHOOL
Department of Science

Memorandum

To: Jean Warden, Librarian
From: Charles Patch, Chairman, Department of Science
Subject: Library Material for the Science Fair

I have just received confirmation from the Superintendent's Office that our proposal for the purchase of library material for next year's fair has been approved. You are authorized to spend up to $600 on books, pamphlets, journals, and other library materials to stimulate ideas for science fair projects. Any photocopying needed may be charged to the Science Department's account.

As previously suggested, these materials could be shelved in a special area of the library for the easy access of interested students. When I return in September, I expect to begin plans for an expanded science fair. These materials and their advance preparation will go a long way to insure that next year's fair will be a greater success than last year's.

The Superintendent thanks you for your efforts in this project. Needless to say, I am in your debt as well.

Chas. Patch

• • • • •

A solution to this case might take the form of a bibliographic essay or an annotated bibliography listing materials to be purchased in support of the science fair at Burford High School.

Indicate which sources should be consulted in order to select the most appropriate books, journals, and other media for prospective science fair entrants. For the faculty? Are there restrictions on the amount or kind of help Miss Warden will be allowed to give prospective science fair participants?

APPENDIX

Scientific periodicals currently received in the Burford High School Library:

The American Biology Teacher
American Forests
Bioscience
Farm Journal
Frontiers
Natural History
Science
Science Peacher
Scientific American
Today's Health

I.
Sample Analysis

BY S. W. BROWN

. . . .

Miss Jean Warden has been assigned the task of collecting materials for her school library "to stimulate ideas for science fair projects," with a budgetary allotment of $600 for the purpose. It is not the intent of this paper to attempt to provide Miss Warden with a ready-made bibliography on science fair projects which can then be transferred to an order list totalling the authorized $600 for the collection. Indeed, such a hasty attempt would have little chance of success in building a useful collection, and it is important to bear in mind that Miss Warden has at least three months in which to work (and probably more, considering that the normal science fair does not really get underway until late in the calendar year). The necessity for a reasonable period of time in which to develop the science fair collection will become evident later. It is rather the purpose of this paper to suggest the various guidelines which should be followed in the selection of suitable material, and to recommend the most helpful sources from which Miss Warden can gain the necessary bibliographic information to make this selection.

First, however, it would be well to put the situation in its proper perspective through a brief examination of the Burford High School's library itself. We note that the library serves a student body of 1,000 students with a collection of 8,950 book titles and 62 journal titles. It takes only a quick look at the latest published standards for high school libraries (or "media centers") to realize that the Burford library falls far short. The 1969 "Standards for School Media Programs" recommend that the book collection should be "at least 6000–10,000 titles representing 10,000 volumes or 20 volumes per student, whichever is greater."[1] Burford, however, has only 8.95 titles per student, or in all only 44.75 percent[2] of the recommended standard. These standards also recommend that a secondary school library subscribe to 125–175 journal titles[3]; Burford receives only 62, or slightly less than one-half of the 1969 standard (at its *minimum* figure). The conclusion we can draw from all this is that the special allotment of $600 should be a welcome one for this substandard school library.[4] To be put to its best use, this funding must be spent carefully.

In order to select the most useful materials for a science fair, the librarian must have a very clear idea of what a science fair *is*, and what it hopes, or should hope, to accomplish. Miss Warden is, of course, not in charge of the fair, but her policy of selection for the fair can go a long way toward assuring that the fair is what it ought to be. The central concept involved here is of course *science*, which James B. Conant has defined as "that portion of accumulated knowledge in which new concepts are continuously developing from *experimentation* and *observation* [italics mine] and lead to further experimenation and observation."[5] These two elements of experimentation and observation are of crucial importance, and unless they are evident in a science project at whatever level of sophistication, the project is not truly scientific and is therefore not in the spirit of a "science" fair.[6] A useful distinction at this point is that between an "experiment" and a "demonstration"; the former being that which sets out to discover (or verify) something and the latter being a predictable process through which one demonstrates a scientific principle or reaction. The high school chemistry teacher who shows his class what happens when he pours sulphuric acid into a beaker of sugar is not performing an "experiment"; yet the student who does the same thing without knowing the result is indeed performing an "experiment," and will learn from his observations. If a science fair is to have as its purpose the encouragement of real science, it must be more than a collection of demonstrational exhibits.

This does not of course mean that everyone participating in a high school science fair must come up with a piece of original scientific research (though this should perhaps be the ultimate goal). But what *is* important is that the student base his project on the "scientific method"—projects that "show cause-and-effect relationships and that make use of validly controlled investigations."[7] A model of a rocket engine or a DNA molecule is not validly scientific, nor is a time-worn demonstration of water displacement. There is no denial that the dividing line between experimentation and demonstration is at times a fine one, and something which later becomes a demonstration was at first an experiment. A convenient distinction, however, might be that an experiment hopes to discover and a demonstration only shows.

Part of the problem as it relates to science fairs is that scientific experiments are on the whole pretty undramatic affairs, and their results not nearly as artistic in the school exhibit as a colorful diagram of the human anatomy, which unfortunately is often the sort of thing which appeals to science fair judges.[8]

For the purposes of our consideration of Miss Warden and her selection policy, we will make the bold assumption that Charles Patch and his Burford colleagues are reasonably enlightened about science fairs and are eager to guide their students toward truly scientific projects. This effort should be reflected in the materials available in the library, and it is obvious that not every book, magazine, or pamphlet which smacks of "science fair" or "experiments you can do" will be suitable. True scientific investigation, however simple, is far more than a process of following directions, and while "books of experiments and examples of past exhibits" have their place, a predominance of them will not lead to the best collection for a science fair. One cannot plunge headlong into an experimental design without first gathering the necessary background knowledge, and thus materials dealing with the various aspects and developments of the sciences themselves are important to our science fair collection. One suspects, in fact, that a separation of "science fair" material from the rest of the science in the Burford library, as suggested by Mr. Patch, would lead to an unhealthy discrimination in the student's mind between the science fair and science itself. (There are, of course, various ways through which the pertinent science materials—including those specifically relating to the fair—could be attractively brought to the notice of the students in the library.) Feeling, then, no compunctions toward spending some of our $600 to enhance the basic science collection—$600 worth of experiments would be an unfortunate waste of money—we can divide the needed materials into two rough categories, the "idea and method" books and the "background research" materials.

Idea and method materials. (See Appendix I for representative examples.) Any project must start with an idea, and the student who wishes to participate in the science fair will need plenty of opportunity to locate an area or problem in which he can discover a genuine interest. For this purpose books of experiments and projects are useful as a starting point. What should be avoided is too much material of the "cookbook" type[9]—detailed plans of experiments which would leave the student little or no room for originality. In fact, experiments designed for a more elementary level have a certain advantage in that they present a simple experiment upon which the high-school student can build a plan of his own. This can also be true of teacher-designed materials for the instruction of basic scientific principles. The UNESCO *Source Book for Science Teaching* (Amsterdam: UNESCO, 1956), for example, is full of literally hundreds of simple "experiments" which, synthesized into a larger experimental plan, can form the basis for worthwhile investigations into any number of fields. Books of experiments, along with those more directly concerned with scientific methodology (such as W. J. Youden's *Experimentation and Measurement*[10]), are helpful in familiarizing the student with the basic techniques and theories of scientific investigation. But it must be borne in mind that these materials should only be the starting point and the student should be encouraged to use his imagination in developing a worthwhile and original project of his own.

Background research materials. The field of this type of material is of course unlimited, and whatever new material is deemed necessary must be acquired with a mind to those basic science books already in the library. This is also an area of selection which should be made in consultation with the teaching staff of the science department. There are a number of helpful series of science books, such as the Science Study Series (Doubleday) and the Westinghouse Search Books (Walker & Co.), which would be particularly useful to a student researching in a particular area for a science project. The emphasis in this area must be on those materials which are not too advanced for the high school student, but which are at the same time sufficiently mature to be informative.

Journals of various types can also be helpful in the initiation and development of science fair projects, and here the teacher's professional journals (such as *The American Biology Teacher* and *The Science Teacher,* already being received by Burford High) are particularly useful. It is a fair assumption that a student will, once he gets deeply into his project, know more in that particular area than his teachers, and their journals can lead him to further information which is nonetheless geared to the level of high school instruction. Other journals, such as *Scientific American,* have "amateur scientist" sections which could prove helpful to a student seeking ideas for a project.

With the general needs of the proposed science fair collection thus in mind, how should Miss Warden go about selecting the most suitable material? Her usual book selection aids will lead her to the standard research materials, but as far as specific materials regarding science fairs, she can easily take advantage of the time she has and write to the various sources which are equipped to handle such matters as part of their services. An explanation of the science fair project and a request for recommended lists of materials would undoubtedly yield a far more current and authoritative bibliography for selection purposes than Miss Warden's own hunting among her own sources. All of the major scientific professional societies (American Chemical Society, American Mathematical Society, etc.) have full-time education directors who are prepared to help out in just such situations (see Appendix II). Institutions such as the Bureau of Educational Research and Field Service (University of Maryland) and the Educational Research Center (M.I.T.) would be willing to help. She should also write to Science Service Inc., which administers the Westinghouse Talent Search (based largely on science fairs), or museums which specialize in science education (e.g., Boston Museum of Science).

It is through agencies such as these that Miss Warden can best seek the professional advice desirable to help her select the most suitable collection for what we hope will be a truly *scientific* science fair at Burford High School.

REFERENCES

1. "The New Standards." *Library Journal* XCIV (October 15, 1969), 3792.
2. Computation to slide-rule accuracy.
3. "The New Standards." *loc. cit.*
4. For example, the total cost of 30 selected titles dealing specifically with science fairs was only $133.13. [Carter, Robert R. comp. "Science Fair Bibliography." *California School Libraries* XL (March 1969) 150–1.]
5. Quoted in Hilary J. Deason. *The AAAS Science Book List for Young Adults.* Washington, D.C.: AAAS, 1964.
6. Sanborn C. Brown, Professor of Physics and Associate Dean of the Graduate School, M.I.T. Interview, Feb. 26, 1970. [Professor Brown was considered something of an authority for the purposes of this paper in that he has participated in the judging of science fairs, has written about and chaired conferences on science education, and has served as chairman of the Lexington School Board.]

7. Edward B. LaNeve. "Are Science Fairs *Really* Science?" *The Science Teacher* XXXIV (December 1967) p. 56.
8. Edwin L. Shay. "Science Fairs, Not Contests." *The Science Teacher* XXXV (April 1968) p. 55.
9. Brown, *loc. cit.*
10. New York: Scholastic Book Service, 1962.

APPENDIX I. EXAMPLES OF "IDEA AND METHOD" MATERIALS

Bacon, W.S., ed. *Ideas for Science Fair Projects*. Arco, 1967.

Brent, Robert. *Chemistry Experiments*. Golden Press, 1963.

Conant, James B. *Harvard Case Histories in Experimental Science*. Harvard, 1957.

———— *Science and Common Sense*. Watts, 1968.

Edison Foundation. *Edison Experiments You Can Do*. Harper, 1960.

Farmer, Robert A. and Sawyer, R. W. *New Ideas for Science Fair Projects*. Arco, 1967.

Herbert, Don. *Mr. Wizard's Science Secrets*. Hawthorn.

Hull, Thomas G. and Jones, Thomas S. *Scientific Exhibits*. Thomas, 1961.

Moore, William. *Your Science Fair Project*. Putnam, 1965.

Pong, Gordon G. *Science Materials*. Brown, 1964.

Podendorf, Illa. *101 Science Experiments*. Childrens, 1960.

Quenouille, Maurice H. *Design and Analysis of Experiment*. Hafner, 1963.

Ruschlis, H. *Discovering Scientific Method*. Harper, 1963.

Science Experimenter. *Junior Science Projects*. Arco, 1967.

Stepp, Ann. *Setting Up a Science Project*. Prentice-Hall, 1966.

Stone, G. K. *Science Projects You Can Do*. Prentice-Hall, 1963.

Strong, C. E., ed. *The Scientific American Book of Projects for the Amateur Scientist*. Simon & Schuster, 1960.

UNESCO. *Source Book for Science Teaching*. UNESCO, 1956.

Welte, Arden. *Your Science Fair*. Burgess, 1956.

Youden, W. J. *Experimentation and Measurement*. Scholastic, 1962.

APPENDIX II. SOURCES FOR MATERIAL
AND BIBLIOGRAPHY ON SCIENCE FAIRS

These professional societies supply useful materials (write c/o Education Director).

American Chemical Society, 1155 16th St. NW, Washington, D.C. 20036

American Institute of Physics, 335 E. 45th St., New York, N.Y. 10017

American Institute of Biological Sciences, 3900 Wisconsin Ave. NW, Washington, D.C. 20016

American Mathematical Society, P.O. Box 6248, Providence, R.I. 02904

American Association for the Advancement of Science, 1515 Massachusetts Ave. NW, Washington, D.C.

National Science Teachers Association, 1201 16th St. NW, Washington, D.C. 20036

Sources of information other than professional societies include the following.

Bureau of Education Research and Field Services (University of Maryland), College Park, Md., 20742

Educational Research Center (M.I.T.), Cambridge, Mass. 02139

Science Service Inc. 1719 N Street NW, Washington, D.C. 20036

II.
Sample Analysis
BY BARBARA MORIARTY

. . . .

Beginning a collection for a science fair takes time. By starting in the summer, the librarian has an excellent opportunity to develop a quite extensive materials center. Since this is a cumulative process, as each year passes, the material available will be more and more comprehensive, and, if conscientiously weeded, more useful. The two basic concepts underlying science fairs are student involvement and scientific exploration. It is the librarian's responsibility to provide adequate background sources and to excite the students' imagination with others.

In order to accomplish the two goals, the librarian must take a survey of the resources already in the library and augment them as completely as her appropriation will allow. Not having direct access to the collection itself, indicative measurements of the adequacy of the library can be derived by comparing the Burford High School (hereafter BHS) with national standards. The Senior High School standards have been revised recently and the comparision of BHS to them is quite informative.

	SCHOOL MEDIA PROGRAM[1]	BHS
Books		
Student	6,000–10,000 titles	
Professional	200–1000 titles	8,950 (combined)
Periodicals		
Student	125–175	
Professional	40–50	62 (combined)

The knowledge that BHS falls far short of the established standards should, however, be tempered by the fact that the library is a fairly new one and is still building. The number of book titles does indicate a collection of almost standard depth, so it should contain enough general science fair materials to support one. Those reference books constituting the absolute minimum would be *Chamber's Technical Dictionary, McGraw-Hill's Encyclopedia of Science and Technology, Van Nostrand's Scientific Encyclopedia, Harper's Encyclopedia of Science, Mathematical Dictionary, McGraw-Hill Yearbook of Science and Technology, Handbook of Chemistry and Physics* and *Hammond's Nature Atlas of America*.[2] Public, research, and college and university libraries usually provide for the more complex needs of the student.[3]

Specific books devoted to science fairs are abundant, although no specific list has been made for senior high schools,[4] and several should be chosen to provide the core. After researching the sources for science books on the high school level (*Senior High School Catalog*,[5] *AAAS Booklist*,[6] *Books in Print 1969*,[7] magazines, and the list compiled by Carter[8]), selected titles will be obvious and immediate purchases (see Appendix I for annotated list of purchases). These books should provide guidance for the student not so much in selecting a specific topic as in the actual purpose and procedure involved in developing an original project. Introduction of the scientific method, laboratory developments and techniques, research patterns and display organization, as well as rules and regulations for the conduct of a student in the fair, present the most essential areas to be covered. The student must be aware of, or have access to, all of the fundamental guidelines concerning the fair. Emphasis on science as opposed to winning artistic design should be reflected in these books.[9] Books should definitely not give recipes, nor should there be many examples of past experiments since originality is so much a part of the whole idea behind a fair.[10] Science fairs should be for scientific experimentation, not historical studies.[11] The problem of nonscientific exhibits results from overanxious teachers who make participation mandatory.[12] If this practice is followed at BHS, the librarian will have to include all science-related fields as well. Even though hard science is being emphasized more and more in fairs,[13] breadth is still the key to science fair acquisitions.

Professional materials should be available to guide the administrators of the fair on application procedures, publicity, judging, exhibition area, program, hostesses, awards and all of the other details.[14] The United States government sends out such articles upon request, especially through agencies such as the National Science Foundation. The *Monthly Catalog* listings of publications are also very helpful in this effort. There will be sections in the books on organizing science fairs, and Miss Warden probably has some on file from the last fair as well.

With basic book materials chosen, the periodical section should be investigated. The collection is already fairly good for science fairs if the journals can be publicized to the point of usefulness. The *Scientific American* has a regular feature, "The Amateur Scientist," which, although it might be too advanced for some, would provide some ideas.[15] *Science* is a little advanced as well, but it is done by the American Association for the Advancement of Science (hereafter AAAS),[16] and might give rise to some original thinking. They are both helpful for book reviews leading to other sources of information. Several of the magazines are not really scientific, such as *Today's Health,* the point being that additional journals are necessary to fill in the collection. A selected list of magazines should be ordered (see Appendix II, the annotated list of magazines) with due thought given to their annual cost. As will be noted by looking at the list, several are professional journals. These are of use not only to teachers, but to the student working on a project, because by the time he gets into the problem in depth, he will need more advanced material and this is one place to locate such articles.[17]

Traditionally, books and periodicals have been the backbone of the library and remain so under most circumstances. Two sources remain unused: films and the vertical file. The Science Museum of Boston[18] has set up a library almost exclusively for science fair materials. They use a great many film loops, as well as thousands of items in their ready reference file. Due to monetary limitation this year, BHS cannot develop both media. It is possible that Miss Warden could use films on science to stimulate interest. She undoubtedly has the catalogs for film companies since teachers use them in the classroom. Even though the individual film loop programs would be a great asset to a media center, this is out of the question for this year at least, and she must stay with the traditional showings. By checking the catalogs, she could find some of interest in the early stages of project development and continue making them more definitive as the science fair approaches. The science department would probably be most happy to suggest some, or could take over that aspect and handle it from the classroom. Several films which might be shown in the library as motivational gimmicks as well as informational items are:

Scientific Method in Action.[19] color, 19 min., $9.00 per day. The
    story of Jonas E. Salk.[20] Mid-high school.
Science Project.[21] b/w, 14 min., $6.00 per day. Story of a boy devel-

oping his own project from idea, through research, plans, and building.[22] High school–college.

Science Fair.[23] color, 14 min., $6.00 per day. Highly motivational film acquainting students, teachers, etc., with science fairs.[24]

Using the Scientific Method.[25] 11 min., $60.00 purchase; rental is available through other agencies. Shows steps.

Prices vary on rentals, but the College Film Center is probably fairly typical in offering the film for three days at one and one-half times the cost and for a week at twice the cost.[26] By checking more catalogs she should no doubt improve on the list, but these or a couple of these would serve as introductory material.

The last area to be discussed is the most important. Up to this time, only about $100 to $150 has been allocated. The rest should be spent in building up a broad-based pamphlet collection including photocopies of important articles from journals, encyclopedias (Americana[27] and Worldbook[28]), and from any other source which might stimulate student thought.

Building a vertical file from nothing is quite a challenge. The tactic is to get on as many mailing lists as possible. As free materials come in, they should be checked carefully and either discarded or filed. When bibliographies or catalogs come, they must be read and materials ordered immediately to avoid getting buried in the paper work. Judgment should be used as the number of copies ordered depends on price and, of course, on estimated need. Those of a more general nature will obviously be in greater demand. Agencies willing to send out materials must number in the thousands (see Appendix III for a very selected list of agencies). Each pamphlet leads to other sources, so careful records should be kept as to those agencies contacted and those who respond.

As each item is added, a filing system will develop with such headings as rules and regulations, criteria for judging, scientific method, exhibition techniques, biology, chemistry, physics, mathematics, for the first influx, and more specific headings as the system expands. The vertical file should be built up over the years to become the major source of science fair materials. To provide the most assistance in the coming year, this is where most money should be spent, including file cabinets if necessary. Science fairs grow from ideas and the vertical file is the best means of stimulation because of its possible scope and currency.

REFERENCES

1. *Standards for School Media Programs.* Chicago: A.L.A., 1969, p. 30.
2. Theodore C. Hines. "Science Reference In Action." *School Libraries.* 13–14 (January 1964) 17.
3. *Edmund Catalog.* Barrington, N.J.: Edmund Scientific Corp., 1969, p. 130.
4. Hines, p. 17.
5. Rachel Stone and E. A. Fidell. *Senior High School Library Catalog.* NY: Wilson, 1967.
6. H. J. Deason. *AAAS Science Booklist for Young Adults.* Washington, D. C.: AAAS, 1964.
7. S. L. Prakken and R. P. Shively, eds. *Subject Guide to Books in Print: An Index to the Publishers' Trade List Annual 1969.* NY: Bowker, 1969, pp. 2667-68.
8. Robert R. Carter. "Science Fair Bibliography." *California School Librarian.* 40 (March 1969) 150–151.
9. E. L. Shay. "Science Fairs, Not Contests." *Science Teacher,* 35 (April 1968) 55.
10. Sanborn C. Brown, B.A., M.A., Ph.D, Professor of Physics and Associate Dean of the Graduate School at M.I.T., *interview* February 26, 1970, 1:00 p.m.
11. Edward B. La Neve. "Are Science Fairs Really Science?" *Science Teacher,* 34 (December 1967) 56.
12. Dael Wolfe. "Science Fairs." *Science.* 140 (June 7, 1963) 55.
13. Sanborn C. Brown, *interview.*
14. Sister M. Pauline, O.S.M. "Planning Your Science Fair." *Catholic School Journal,* 64 (September 1964) 54.
15. Sanborn C. Brown, *interview.*
16. Bill Katz and Berry Gargal. *Magazines for Libraries.* NY: Bowker, 1969, p. 318.
17. Sanborn C. Brown, *interview.*
18. *Science Museum,* Science Park, Boston.
19. *College Film Catalog.* Chicago, Illinois. p. 62.
20. *International Film Bureau Inc., Catalog.* Chicago, Illinois, p. 78.
21. *College Film Center,* p. 62.
22. *International Film Bureau,* p. 78.
23. *College Film Center,* p. 62.

24. *International Film Bureau,* p. 78.
25. *Coronet Films Catalog,* Sales Department, Chicago, Illinois, 1967–68, p. 105.
26. *College Film Center,* p. 62.
27. Fergus J. Wood. "Scientific Method." *Encyclopedia Americana International.* NY: Americana Corp., vol. 24, 1969, pp. 418–21.
28. H. Craig Sype. "Science—'Science Projects'." *World Book Encyclopedia.* Chicago: Field Enterprises Education Corp., vol. 17, 1969, p. 175.

ADDITIONAL SOURCES

Encyclopedia of Associations: National Organizations of the United States. Gale Research Co., Detroit, 1968.
Enrichment—Classroom Challenge. Superintendent of Public Instruction, Columbus, Ohio: Holt, 1966.
"New Standards for School Libraries." *Louisiana Library Association Bulletin.* 31 (Winter, 1969) 127–129.
Standards for School Library Programs. American Association of School Libraries, Division of the American Library Association. Chicago: ALA, 1960 pp. 119, 127.
United States Department of Health Education and Welfare 1967 Annual Report. Washington, D.C.: GPO, 1967.
United States Government Organization Manual 1969–70. National Archives and Records, General Services Administration, Washington, D.C.

APPENDIX I

The following books are recommended for immediate purchase. The symbols used follow the price and precede any annotation: SHS, in *Senior High School Catalog;* IP, in print; AAAS, in *AAAS Science Booklist for Young Adults;* SFB, in Carter's "Science Fair Bibliography" (see reference 8); G , grade level; *, two copies to be purchased.

Barrett, Raymond E. *Build it Yourself Science Laboratory.* Doubleday, 1962. $5.95 AAAS, IP, SFB, G-7+

> "A detailed guide to equipment and facilities for individual student research at home, or in a school that does not have a standard well-equipped laboratory. A separate section is provided for each major scientific discipline, to which is appended a list of suggestions for student investigations." (AAAS p. 9)

Benrey, Ronald and other winners of the National Science Fair-International. *Ideas for Science Fair Projects.* Arco, 1963. $2.50 SHS

> Partial Contents: a history of science fairs; choosing a topic; types of projects; documentation; research; shopping; building your project; project section (articles by students); criteria for judging the National Science Fair-International; rules for regional or school science fairs; regulations for experiments with animals; lists of suppliers. (SHS, p. 102)

Conant, James Bryant et al. *Harvard Case Histories in Experimental Science.* 2 volumes, Harvard University Press, 1957. $10.00 SHS, IP

> "These books provide the reader with a real appreciation of the scientist at work." with bibliography. (AAAS) This is a fairly old book but still has use in developing thought patterns which might lead to original thought.

Conant, James Bryant. *Science and Common Sense.* Watts, 1968. $6.71 SHS, IP

> Bibliography and "what scientists can accomplish and how they work." *(Library Journal)*

Deason, Hilary J. and Robert W. Lynn. *An Inexpensive Science Library.* (5th edition) Washington, D.C.: AAAS 1961. $.25

> A selected list of some 400 paperback science books. These might be purchased by the individual student in his particular area. At least this would give him access to such a thought.

> *Evaluation of Existing Criteria for Judging Quality of Science Exhibits* (with bibliographies)

Monthly Catalog #8295 p. 11, Clearinghouse. $1.00*

> This is a pamphlet needed by both administration and student.

Harbeck, Richard. *Exploring Science in Your Home Laboratory.* NY: 4 Winds Press, 1966. $3.27 SFB, IP, G-7–11

> Simple, detailed plans for setting up and equipping an inexpensive home science laboratory with drawings and photographs by the author. *(Library Journal)*

Holden, Alan. *Crystals and Crystal Growing.* Doubleday, 1960. $1.46 AAAS, SFB, IP, G- junior high +

> It is a beautiful book with information on one field of continuing interest to many age groups. Its real importance lies in the fact that it is part of the Science Study Series which should probably be bought in its entirety when the opportunity arises.

Ruchlis, Hy. *Discovering Scientific Method.* Harper, 1963. SHS, SFB

> "Although the reader is asked to devise his own questions, the author poses excellent ones and demonstrates how to bring the problem to logical conclusions." *(Library Journal)*

Sawyer, Roger W. and Robert A. Farmer. *New Ideas for Science Fair Projects.* NY: Arco, 1967. $3.95 SHS, IP, G- 7–12

> "A reference book of ideas for science projects . . . as well as a list of rules, topics to choose from and display techniques." *(Book Buyer's Guide)*

Stong, C. E. ed. *The Scientific American Book of Projects for the Amateur Scientist.* Simon and Schuster, 1960. $6.95 SHS, SFB, AAAS, IP

> "The most explicit how-to-do-it book currently in print which will acquaint students with the essentials of the scientific method and assist them in beginning their own research studies. Examples in all major disciplines." (AAAS, p. 12)

UNESCO. *700 Science Experiments for Everyone.* Rev. and enl. ed. Doubleday, 1962. $4.50 SHS, SFB, IP

Some of the experiments might be too elementary, but would provide basic materials.

Welte, Arden F. *Your Science Fair*. Minneapolis: Burgess Pub., Co., 1962. $3.50
IP also in Science Museum in Boston as a well-used book. This is a guide to successful science exhibits and helps to acquaint the student with the criteria used in judging science fairs.

APPENDIX II

As additional resource material for encouraging creativity, as well as for continuing value in the library, the following magazines are recommended if the budget will allow their subscription to be continued. The brief annotations which follow the titles are from Katz' book *Magazines for Libraries;* the page number is noted at the end of the annotation.

Chemistry. American Chemical Society. $4.00
To further the educational end, special departments are included such as "Lab Bench," which describes experiments which have been and can be undertaken at the high school level. An exceptional title for high school libraries. p. 76

Endeavor. free
Intended to record and review the progress of science. Highly recommended for most libraries. p. 315

Journal of Chemical Education. $4.00
Should be found in every high school library. p. 78

Mathematics Teacher. $5.00
Reports of research or descriptions of new experiments are included. p. 245

Physics Teacher. $5.00
Brief communication blurbs on classroom techniques, lab demonstrations, new equipment, tips on improvements, etc. directed to the high school level. p. 284

Physics Today. $4.00
Highly recommended for any public or High School library that would like to acquire more than a general science periodical. p. 284

Sea Frontiers. free
A first choice for most libraries. p. 118

Sky and Telescope. $6.00
Leading astronomy magazine for beginners regardless of educational or age level. p. 34

APPENDIX III

Organizations offering material useful in setting up a science fair collection are listed on the following pages.

I. ORGANIZATIONS

American Association for the Advancement
of Science
1515 Massachusetts Ave., N.W.
Washington, D.C.

American Association of Physics Teachers
(Under the American Institute of Physics)
1201 16th St., N.W.
Washington, D.C.   20036

American Chemical Society
1155 16th St., N.W.
Washington, D.C.   20036

American Heart Association
44 E. 23rd St.
New York, New York

American Humane Society
180 Longwood Ave.
Boston, Massachusetts

American Institute of Biological Sciences
2000 P St., N.W.
Washington, D.C.

American Institute of Physics
335 E. 45th St.
New York, New York

American Mathematical Society
P.O. Box 6248
Providence, R.I.   02904

American Pharmaceutical Association
2215 Constitution Ave., N.W.
Washington, D.C.   20037

Chamber of Commerce of the United States
1615 H St., N.W.
Washington, D.C.

Engineers Council for Professional
Development
29 W. 39th St.
New York, New York

The Institute of Natural Science
University of North Carolina
Chapel Hill, North Carolina

Junior Engineering Technical Society
P.O. Box 598
East Lansing, Michigan

Minnesota Academy of Science
51 University Ave.
St. Paul, Minnesota

National Academy of Sciences
National Resource Council
2101 Constitution Ave.
Washington, D.C.

National Association of Biology Teachers
1420 N St., N.W.
Washington, D.C.   20550

National Association of Geology Teachers
Department of Geology
City College
New York, N.Y.   10031

National Council of Teachers of Mathematics
1201 16th St., N.W.
Washington, D.C.   20036

National Health Council
1790 Broadway
New York, New York

National Science Foundation
1800 G St., N.W.
Washington, D.C.   20550

National Science Teachers Association
(Future Scientists of America)
1201 16th St., N.W.
Washington, D.C.   20036

National Society of Professional Engineers
2029 K St., N.W.
Washington, D.C.

Science Service
(Science Clubs of America)
1719 N St., N.W.
Washington, D.C.   20036

Thomas Alva Edison Foundation
8 W. 40th St.
New York, New York

UNESCO Publications
801 3rd Ave.
New York, New York

II.   GOVERNMENT PUBLICATIONS

Clearinghouse
U.S. Department of Commerce
Springfield, Va.   22151

Food and Drug Administration
200 C St., S.W.
Washington, D.C.   20204

U.S. Atomic Energy Commission
P.O. Box 62
Oak Ridge, Tenn.   37831

Superintendent of Documents
U.S.G.P.O.
Washington, D.C.

U.S. Department of Agriculture
14th St. and Independence Ave., S.W.
Washington, D.C.   20250

U.S. Department of Health Education and
   Welfare
Office of Education
400 Maryland Ave., S.W.
Washington, D.C.   20202

U.S. Department of the Interior-
Geological Survey
18th and F Streets, N.W.
Washington, D.C.   20242

III.   INDUSTRY

American Gas Association, Inc.
605 3rd Ave.
New York, N.Y.   10016

American Petroleum Institute
1271 Ave. of the Americas
New York, N.Y.   10020

Charles Pfizer and Co., Inc.
Educational Services Dept.
235 E. 42nd St.
New York, New York

Eastman Kodak Co.
Consumer Markets Division
Rochester, N.Y.   14650

Esso Research and Engineering Co.
P.O. Box 45
Linden, N.J.   17036

FMC Corporation
American Viscose Division
1617 John F. Kennedy Blvd.
Philadelphia, Pa.   19103

Manufacturing Chemists' Association
1825 Connecticut Ave., N.W.
Washington, D.C.

Standard Oil Co.
Education Division
15 W. 51st St.
New York, New York

IV.   MUSEUMS

American Museum of Natural History
Dept. of Education
Central Park West at 79th St.
New York, New York

Museum of Science
Science Park
Boston, Massachusetts

Oregon Museum of Science & Industry
4015 S.W. Canyon Rd.
Portland, Oregon

Smithsonian Institution
Publications Distribution Section
Washington, D.C.

V.   DEALERS AND SUPPLIERS CATALOGS

Allied Radio
100 N. Western Ave.
Chicago, Ill.   60680

American Type Culture Collection
12301 Parklawn Drive
Rockville, Md.   20852

Bio Metal Associates
Bio Quip Products
P.O. Box 61
Santa Monica, Cal.   90409

The Ealing Corporation
2225 Massachusetts Ave.
Cambridge, Mass.   02140

Edmund Scientific Co.
101 East Gloucester Pike
Barrington, N.J.   08007

Macalaster Scientific Corp.
186 3rd Ave.
Waltham, Mass.   02154

Pacific Bio Marine
P.O. Box 536
Venice, Cal.   90921

Radio Shack-Durrell
920 Main St.
Waltham, Mass.   02154

Turtox Biological Supplies
General Biological Supply House
8200 S. Hoyne Ave.
Chicago, Ill.   60620

Appendix: Pathfinders

· · · · · · · · · · · · · · · ·

The concept of library Pathfinders was originated with Charles H. Stevens, Associate Director for Library Development, Project Intrex, Massachusetts Institute of Technology, and was developed by the staff of the Model Library Project of Project Intrex under a grant from the Council on Library Resources. Pathfinders are designed to help library users begin to locate published materials on very specific subjects, with which the users have little or only general familiarity. Each of the approximately 150 issues currently in print is similar in style and arrangement to the three that follow.

During the spring of 1970, a cooperative program of Pathfinder compilation was arranged between the Model Library Project Staff and the School of Library Science at Simmons College. Initially, students in the Literature of Science and Technology course were assigned the preparation of Pathfinders for topics suggested by the staff of the Model Library Project. Because of the proximity of Simmons to Massachusetts Institute of Technology, the students were directed to work with the Barker Engineering Library. As Pathfinder topics became more diverse, student access to the Science Library at Massachusetts Institute of Technology and the Countway Library of Medicine, Harvard University, was arranged. Simmons students are currently compiling Pathfinders in mathematics, physics, chemistry, biology, metallurgy, ecology, engineering (including biomedical engineering), and medicine.

In 1970–1971, graduate students at Simmons prepared, and submitted for possible publication, eighty Pathfinders. Nearly fifty of the student Pathfinders have been published. Since this cooperative program was first established with Simmons, thirteen additional schools of library science and nine university and special libraries have joined it. The only necessary prerequisite for Pathfinder production is the use of a working collection with strengths in the chosen Pathfinder topics.

For the student of the literature of science and technology, compiling a Pathfinder requires making effective use of a variety of forms of the literature, thus simulating the task of the professional science reference specialist. The author has found close parallels between the use of the problem-centered approach to instruction and the preparation of a Pathfinder. For example, the solution of a case study and the preparation of a Pathfinder both involve a search of the literature, the location of the most pertinent sources for citation, and the presentation of a solution to the problem. Like the solution to a case, the Pathfinder assignment necessitates consultation of scientific and technical sources in a specific problem context.

In assigning a Pathfinder project to a student, I have elected to place the student on his own after a topic is selected, and after he has received the guidelines, which have been prepared by and are available from the Model Library Project. It has been my practice to assign Pathfinder topics during the first or second class meeting and have them due as class assignments four weeks later. Other class and case work continues during the period of Pathfinder preparation.

The three Pathfinders included in this Appendix are examples of student-produced compilations published and distributed by the Model Library Project. These Pathfinders, as all others produced by Simmons students, have been reviewed and revised both by the instructor and the staff of the Model Library Project. On the reverse of each Pathfinder, credit is given to both the student and his institution upon publication. Although the work involved in compilation of a Pathfinder may represent a challenge of some magnitude to the student, the personal and professional pride of each student-author is great. In this manner, the student of the scientific and technical literature has the satisfaction of knowing his work is made available to the users of many libraries by the Model Library Project. In addition, the student's knowledge of the literature of a specific subject area in many of its forms is enhanced because of this assignment.

The author is grateful to Mr. Charles H. Stevens, Associate Director for Reader Services of Project Intrex, and to Mr. Jeffrey J. Gardner and Miss Marie P. Canfield, both of the Model Library Project Staff, for their continued guidance and consultation in the cooperative program of Pathfinder development.

Further information on library Pathfinders is available from the Model Library Project of Project Intrex at Massachusetts Institute of Technology and in the *Semiannual Activity Reports of Project Intrex* for September 15, 1971 (pp. 66 ff). Subsequent issues of this publication will contain further reports on library Pathfinders of this type and others still in the experimental stage.

I. MICROWAVES

SCOPE: Electromagnetic waves whose frequencies
are bounded by those of radio waves and infrared waves.

An introduction to this topic appears in the
*McGraw-Hill Encyclopedia of Science and
Technology*, vol. 8, pp. 412–416, under the
entry "Microwave."
Q121 .M147 1966 v. 8   5th Floor

BOOKS dealing with microwaves are listed in
the subject card catalog. Look for the subjects:
"Microwaves" (highly relevant)
"Wave Motion, Theory of" (more general)

Frequently mentioned texts include:

Atwater, Harry A.
Introduction to Microwave Theory (1962)
QC661 .A887   7th Floor

Collin, Robert E.
Foundations for Microwave Engineering (1966)
TK7870 .C699   7th Floor

Fuller, A. J. Baden
Microwaves (1969)
TK7876 .F965   7th Floor

Lance, Algie L.
*Introduction to Microwave Theory and
Measurements* (1964)
TK7870 .L246   7th Floor

Reich, Herbert J., et al.
Microwave Theory and Techniques (1953)
TK7870 .R347   7th Floor

Other books including material on microwaves
are shelved under call numbers: QC661,
TK7870 and TK7876.

HANDBOOKS, ENCYCLOPEDIAS, and
DICTIONARIES which contain information on
microwaves are:

Harvey, Arthur F.
Microwave Engineering (1963)
TK7870 H341   7th Floor

Sucher, M. and Fox, J. (eds.)
Handbook of Microwave Measurements 3d ed.
(1963)
TK6553 .S942   5th Floor

BIBLIOGRAPHIES which contain material on
microwaves include:

Microwave Journal, January 1, 1967,
"Microwave Engineers' Technical and Buyers'
Guide Edition," Bibliography, pp. 15–272
(Covers 1946–1965 literature)   6th Floor

Microwave Journal, February 1, 1969,
"Microwave Engineers' Technical and Buyers'
Guide Edition," pp. 202–214; see especially
"Microwave Theory" pp. 209–210 (Covers 1967
literature)
TK7870 .M626 1969   5th Floor

U.S. National Aeronautics and Space
Administration. Scientific and Technical
Information Division. *Lasers and Masers: A
Continuing Bibliography*. (1962–1967) (NASA
SP–7009 & supplements)
TL521 .A333 no. 7009   5th Floor

Becker, P. W. and Warren, S.E.
Bibliography on Masers, 1954–1961, and
Supplement, 1961–1963.
ZTK7872 .M3 .B396   5th Floor

JOURNAL ARTICLES and other literature on
microwaves are indexed primarily in the guides
listed. The quoted subject headings are those in
use since 1965 unless other dates are given.

*Library Pathfinders—designed to help users begin to locate published information in specific fields—are prepared
under a grant from the Council on Library Resources by the staff of Project Intrex, Massachusetts Institute of
Technology.* © *1970 Massachusetts Institute of Technology, Cambridge, Massachusetts. All rights reserved.*

Applied Science and Technology Index (Covers popular engineering periodicals) See:
"Microwaves" (1970+; highly relevant)
"Spectrum, Microwave" (also relevant)
ZT45 .A652   5th Floor

Engineering Index (Covers 2,000+ professional journals) See:
"Electron tubes—Microwave" (highly relevant)
"Masers" (also relevant)
"Electromagnetic waves" (more general)
ZTA145 .E57   5th Floor

Science Abstracts. Series B. Electrical and Electronics Abstracts (1966+; earlier, see *Section B. Electrical Engineering Abstracts*) See:
"Microwave devices" (relevant)
"Masers" (also relevant)
"Microelectronics" (more general)
ZTK146 .E38   5th Floor

International Aerospace Abstracts (Covers aero-astro literature) See:
"Microwaves"
ZTL790 .I61   5th Floor

Electronics and Communications Abstracts (Covers world literature) See:
"Microwave . . ."
ZTK5101 .E38   5th Floor

Other indexes, listed here, should be used for an exhaustive search. Only a limited return can be expected for the time spent. Directions are generally given in the front of each issue.

Chemical Abstracts
ZQD31 .C517   5th Floor

Dissertation Abstracts International Section B. The Sciences and Engineering
Z5055 .U49 .D61   5th Floor

Pandex Current Index to Scientific and Technical Literature
ZQ158 .P189   5th Floor

Science Abstracts. Series A. Physics Abstracts
ZQC21 .P5783   5th Floor

Science Citation Index
ZQ158 .S416   5th Floor

JOURNALS that often contain articles relevant to microwaves are:

Microwave Journal   6th Floor

Institute of Electrical and Electronics Engineers. Transactions on Microwave Theory and Techniques   6th Floor

Journal of Applied Physics   6th Floor

Journal of Microwave Power   6th Floor

STATE-OF-THE-ART REVIEWS and CONFERENCE PROCEEDINGS containing material on microwaves include:

Advances in Microwaves (1966+)
TK7870 .A2445   7th Floor

Group on Microwave Theory and Techniques (G.—M.T.T.) International Microwave Symposium.
Program and Digest (1961+)
TK7800 .G111   7th Floor

European Microwave Conference, 1969.
Proceedings.
TK7876 .E89 1969   7th Floor

Southworth, George C., "Survey and History of the Progress of the Microwave Arts," *Institute of Radio Engineers. Proceedings*, May, 1962, pp. 1199-1206.   6th Floor

REPORTS and other types of literature are indexed in these guides:

U.S. Government Research and Development Reports (Index) (1968+) (Covers U.S. sponsored reports) See:
"Microwave(s) . . ." (highly relevant)
"Maser . . ." (also relevant)
ZQ180 .U5 .U581   5th Floor

U.S. NASA Scientific and Technical Aerospace Reports—STAR (Covers worldwide report literature) See:
"Microwaves" (highly relevant)
"Masers . . ." (also relevant)
ZTL790 .U586   5th Floor

This Pathfinder was compiled by Joan Tomkins, Simmons College School of Library Science, Boston, Massachusetts, and edited by the Project Intrex Model Library staff at M.I.T. Comments and additions may be sent to Pathfinder Editor, Project Intrex, Room 10–400, M.I.T., Cambridge, Massachusetts 02139.

II. INTEGRATED CIRCUITS

SCOPE: Combination of interconnected active and passive circuit elements inseparably associated on or within a continuous substrate and capable of performing a circuit function.

An introduction to this topic appears in *Encyclopaedic Dictionary of Physics*, J. Thewlis (ed.) suppl. v. 2, pp. 128–129 (1967) under the entry "Integrated Circuits."
QC5 .E56 suppl. v. 2 1967   5th Floor

BOOKS dealing with integrated circuits are listed in the subject card catalog. Look for the subjects:
"Integrated Circuits" (highly relevant)
"Microwaves" (also relevant)

Frequently mentioned texts include:

Camenzind, Hans R.
Circuit Design for Integrated Electronics (1968)
TK7874 .C181   7th Floor

Doyle, John M.
Thin-Film and Semiconductor Integrated Circuitry (1966)
TK7874 .D754   7th Floor

Integrated Circuit Engineering Corp.
Integrated Circuit Engineering. Basic Technology (1966)
TK7870 .I615 1966   7th Floor

Motorola, Inc. Semiconductor Products Div.
Integrated Circuits: Design Principles and Fabrication (1965)
TK7870 .M919   7th Floor

Motorola, Inc. Semiconductor Products Div.
Analysis and Design of Integrated Circuits (1967)
TK7874 .M919   7th Floor

Radio Corporation of America
RCA Linear Integrated Circuits (1967)
TK7870 .R129 1967   7th Floor

Other books including material on integrated circuits are shelved under call numbers TK7874 and TK7870.

HANDBOOKS, ENCYCLOPEDIAS, and DICTIONARIES which contain information on integrated circuits are:

McGraw-Hill Encyclopedia of Science and Technology (1966) v. 8, pp. 350–351.
Q121 .M147 1966 v. 8   5th Floor

Hughes, L. E. C. and Holland, F. W. (eds.)
Handbook of Electronic Engineering, 3d. ed. (1967) pp. 598–603.
TK7825 .H893 1967   5th Floor

Hunter, Lloyd P. *Handbook of Semiconductor Electronics* (1970) Section 1.17, 5, 8, and 10.
TK7871.85 .H945 1970   5th Floor

Thomas, Harry E. *Handbook of Transistors, Semiconductors, Instruments, and Microelectronics* (1968) pp. 364–391.
TK7871.85 .T457   5th Floor

Gibson, Robert E. (ed.) *Integrated Circuits Handbook* (1966)
TK7870 .G4495   5th Floor

Digital Integrated Circuit D.A.T.A. Book, 12th ed., Spring, 1971.
TK7888.3 .D5745 Spring 1971   5th Floor

Linear Integrated Circuits D.A.T.A. Book, 5th ed., Spring, 1971.
TK7867 .D433 Spring 1971   5th Floor

Anglo-American Microelectronics Data, 1968–1969. 2 vols.
TK7805 .A589 1968/69   5th Floor

Gans, F. *Linear Integrated Circuits; Testing and Application*
TK7874 .G199   7th Floor

American Society for Testing and Materials. *1970 Book of A.S.T.M. Standards. Part 8* (Includes standards on Materials for Electron Devices and Microelectronics; F-series)
TA401 .A5173 1969 v. 8   5th Floor

Library Pathfinders—designed to help users begin to locate published information in specific fields—are prepared under a grant from the Council on Library Resources by the staff of Project Intrex, Massachusetts Institute of Technology. © *1970 Massachusetts Institute of Technology, Cambridge, Massachusetts. All rights reserved.*

BIBLIOGRAPHIES which contain material on integrated circuits include:

Henle, R. P. and Hill, L. O., "Integrated Computer Circuits . . ." *IEEE Proceedings,* v. 54 (Dec., 1966) p. 1860 (43 references)   6th Floor

U.S. Defense Documentation Center. *DDC Bibliography on Microminiaturization (Electronics)* v. 1 (1969) (AD684300) See pp. D6–D7, "Integrated Circuits" (22 refs.) ZTK7874 .U58 v.1   7th Floor

JOURNAL ARTICLES and other literature on integrated circuits are indexed primarily in the guides listed. The quoted subject headings are those in use since 1965 unless other dates are given.

Applied Science and Technology Index "Electronic circuits, Integrated" (1970 +) "Electronic circuits—Integrated circuits" (1967–69) "Electronic circuits—Miniaturization" (1956–66) ZT45 .A652   5th Floor

Engineering Index See: "Integrated Circuits" (1966 +) "Radio Circuits—Miniature" (1965) ZT145 .E57   5th Floor

Science Abstracts. Series B. Electrical and Electronics Abstracts (1966 +) See: "Integrated circuit(s) . . ." (1969 +) "Microelectronics/Integrated circuits" (1966–1968) ZTK145 .E57   5th Floor

International Aerospace Abstracts See: "Integrated Circuit(s)" ZTL790 .I61   5th Floor

Science Abstracts. Series C. Computer and Control Abstracts (1969 +) See: "Integrated circuits" ZQA402.3 .C764   5th Floor

The following indexes should be used for an exhaustive search. Only a limited return can be expected. Directions are generally given in the front of each issue.

Dissertation Abstracts International. Section B. The Sciences and Engineering Z5055 .U49 .D61   5th Floor

Pandex Current Index to Scientific and Technical Literature ZQ158 .P189   5th Floor

JOURNALS that often contain articles relevant to integrated circuits are:

IEEE Journal of Solid State Circuits 6th Floor

IEEE Transactions on Electron Devices 6th Floor

Microelectronics and Reliability   6th Floor

STATE-OF-THE-ART REVIEWS and CONFERENCE PROCEEDINGS containing material on integrated circuits include:

Johnson, H. "The Anatomy of I-C Technology," *Spectrum,* v. 7 (Feb., 1970) pp. 56–66. 6th Floor

IEEE International Solid-State Circuits Conference, *Digest* (1959 +) TK7870 .I61   7th Floor

Conference on Integrated Circuits, 1967. (IEE Conference Publication No. 30) TK7874 .C748 1967   7th Floor

Integrated Circuits Seminar, Stevens Institute of Technology (1967 +) TK7874 .I61   7th Floor

REPORTS and other types of literature are indexed in these guides:

U.S. Government Research and Development Reports (Index) (1968 +) (Covers U.S. sponsored reports) See: "Integrated Circuit(s)" ZQ180 .U5 .U581   5th Floor

U.S. NASA Scientific and Technical Aerospace Reports—STAR (Worldwide report literature) See: "Integrated Circuit(s)" ZTL790 .U586   5th Floor

This Pathfinder was compiled by Susan N. Bjørner, Simmons College School of Library Science, Boston, Massachusetts, and edited by the Project Intrex Model Library staff at M.I.T. Comments and additions may be sent to Pathfinder Editor, Project Intrex, Room 10–400, M.I.T., Cambridge, Massachusetts 02139.

III. WATER POLLUTION—
RADIOACTIVE MATERIALS

SCOPE: The incidence of radioactive materials in water—
caused by industrial and military facilities, nuclear accident,
or weapons testing—in amounts above the natural concentration.

An introduction to this topic appears in
Mawson, Colin A., *Management of Radioactive
Wastes* (1965) pp. 125–134.
TD898 .M462   Science Library

BOOKS dealing with radioactive water pollution
are listed in the subject card catalog. Look for
the subjects:
"Radioactive Waste Disposal" (relevant)
"Water–Pollution" (more general)
"Radioactivity" (related)

Frequently mentioned texts include:

Eisenbud, Merril
Environmental Radioactivity (1963) pp.
112–131.
RA569 .E36   Science Library

International Atomic Energy Agency
*Disposal of Radioactive Wastes Into Fresh
Water* (1963) (I.A.E.A. Safety Series No. 10)
HD9698.5 .A2 .S128 no.10   Science

International Atomic Energy Agency
Radioactive-Waste Disposal Into the Sea (1961)
(I.A.E.A. Safety Series No. 5)
HD9698.5 .A2 .S128 no.5   7th Floor (also
in Science Library)

Straub, Conrad P.
Low-Level Radioactive Wastes (1964)
TD898 .S912   7th Floor

Other books including material on radioactive
water pollution are shelved under call numbers
RA569, TD420–TD425, and TD897–TD898.

HANDBOOKS which contain information on
radioactive water pollution are:

Etherington, Harold (ed.) *Nuclear Engineering
Handbook* (1958) pp. 7–52 to 7–54 and
11–140 to 11–145.

TK9151 .E84   5th Floor (Also in Science
Library—Reference)

Reactor Handbook, 2d ed. (1960–1964) v. 1,
pp. 19–20; v. 4, pp. 436, 455–456.
TK9202 .R281   Science Library—Reference

BIBLIOGRAPHIES which contain material on
radioactive water pollution include:

International Atomic Energy Agency. *Disposal
of Radioactive Waste into Marine and Fresh
Waters* (1962) (I.A.E.A. Bibliography Series
No. 5) (1906 references)
ZHD9698 .A1 .I611 no. 5   7th Floor (Also
in Science Library)

Stewart, R. Keith, et al. *Water Pollution
Control, Waste Treatment, and Water
Treatment* (1966) pp. 24, 69–72 (66 refs.)
ZTD425 .S851   7th Floor

"Review of the Literature on Wastewater and
Water Pollution Control," compiled annually in
Water Pollution Control Federation. Journal
(See June issue under the heading "Industrial
Wastes—Radioactive")   6th Floor

JOURNAL ARTICLES and other literature on
radioactive water pollution are indexed primarily
in the guides listed. The quoted subject headings
are those in use since 1965 unless other dates
are given.

Applied Science and Technology Index (Covers
popular engineering periodicals) See:
"Water Pollution—Radioactive Pollution"
(highly relevant)
"Radioactive Water Disposal" (more general)
ZT45 .A652   5th Floor (Also in Science
Library)

Engineering Index (Covers 2,000+ professional
journals) See:

*Library Pathfinders—designed to help users begin to locate published information in specific fields—are prepared
under a grant from the Council on Library Resources by the staff of Project Intrex, Massachusetts Institute of
Technology © 1970 Massachusetts Institute of Technology, Cambridge, Massachusetts. All rights reserved.*

"Water Pollution—Radioactive Materials"
(highly relevant)
"Industrial Wastes—Radioactive Materials"
(more general)
ZTA145 .E57   5th Floor (Also in Science
Library)

Pollution Abstracts (1970+) (Covers
international journal and report literature) See:
"Radioactive . . ."
ZTD180 .P777   5th Floor (Also in Science
Library)

Great Britain, Department of Scientific and
Industrial Research. *Water Pollution Abstracts.*
See:
"Radioactive . . ." (highly relevant)
"Radioactivity" (highly relevant)
ZTD420 .G787   5th Floor

Other indexes, listed here, should be used for an
exhaustive search. Only a limited return can
be expected for the time spent. Directions are
generally given in the front of each issue.

Water Resources Abstracts
ZTD201 .W314   5th Floor

Chemical Abstracts
ZQD31 .C517   5th Floor (Also in Science
Library)

Science Citation Index
ZQ158 .S416   5th Floor (Also in Science
Library)

*Dissertation Abstracts International. Section B.
The Sciences and Engineering*
Z5055 .U49 .D61   5th Floor (Also in
Humanities Library)

JOURNALS that often contain articles relevant
to radioactive water pollution are:

*Water Pollution Control Association.
Journal*   6th Floor

Nuclear Safety
TK .N962   Science Library

Health Physics
RC .H434   Science Library

STATE-OF-THE-ART REVIEWS and
CONFERENCE PROCEEDINGS containing
material on radioactive water pollution include:

Parker, Frank L. "Status of Radioactive Waste
Disposal in U.S.A." *American Society of Civil
Engineers. Proceedings. Journal of the Sanitary
Engineering Division,* v. 95, no. SA3, (June
1969), pp. 439–464 (60 references).
6th Floor

Scientific Conference on the Disposal of
Radioactive Wastes, 1959. *Disposal of
Radioactive Wastes.* (1960) 2 volumes.
TD812 .S416   7th Floor

International Conference on the Peaceful Uses of
Atomic Energy, 3rd, 1964. *Proceedings* (1965)
v. 14, pp. 62–106.
QC770 .I616 1964 v. 14   7th Floor (Also in
Science Library)

Symposium on the Disposal of Radioactive
Wastes into Seas, Oceans, and Surface Waters,
1966. *Proceedings* (1966)
TD898 .S9894   7th Floor

REPORTS and other types of literature are
indexed in these guides:

*U.S. Government Research and Development
Reports (Index)* (1968+) (Covers U.S.
sponsored reports) See:
"Radioactive Waste" (general)
"Water Pollution" (general)
ZQ180 .U5 .U581   5th Floor (Also in
Science Library)

*U.S. NASA Scientific and Technical Aerospace
Reports—STAR* (Worldwide report literature)
See:
"Radioactive Contamination" (prior to 1967;
general)
"Radioactive Contaminants" (1968+; general)
"Water Pollution" (1969+; general)
ZTL790 .U586   5th Floor (Also in Science
Library)

U.S. Atomic Energy Commission.
Nuclear Science Abstracts (International
coverage) See:
"Water—radioactive contamination . . ."
"Water—radioactivity . . ."
"Sea Water—radioactive contamination . . ."
"Sea Water—radioactivity . . ."
"Radioactive Contamination"
ZQC776 .U5851   5th Floor (Also in Science
Library)

This Pathfinder was compiled by Hilary A. Wayson, Simmons College School of Library Science, Boston,
Massachusetts, and edited by the Project Intrex Model Library staff at M.I.T. Comments and additions
may be sent to Pathfinder Editor, Project Intrex, Room 10–400, M.I.T., Cambridge, Massachusetts
02139.